# CELTIC
# DESIGN

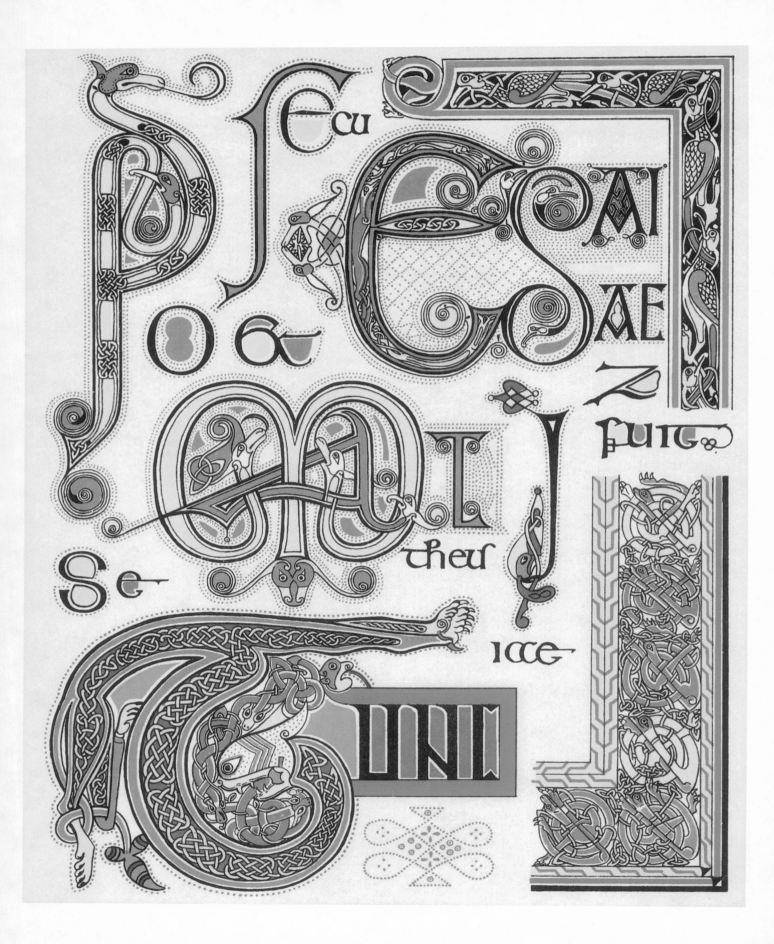

# CELTIC DESIGN

## A Sourcebook of Patterns and Motifs

Iain Zaczek

STUDIO
EDITIONS

First published in 1995 by Studio Editions Ltd,
Princess House, 50 Eastcastle Street, London W1N 7AP, England

Picture research by Vanessa Fletcher

Designed by SPL Design, London

Printed and bound in the UK

ISBN 1 85891 247 4

# Contents

Frontispiece: Decorated lettering from Celtic manuscripts featured in this book, including the Book of Kells and the Lindisfarne Gospels.

Copyright page: Delicate designs taken mainly from the Lindisfarne Gospels, seventh century.

# Introduction

Celtic design is remarkable both for its resilience and its versatility. The original Celts flourished more than 2000 years ago, but elements of the style they created have endured and can be seen on everyday objects all around us as well as in historical documents and ancient artefacts.

The Celtic peoples appear to have originated in Central Europe, although their influence eventually spread to most parts of the continent. They never established a clearly-defined empire, in the way that the Greeks and Romans did, and they were known by a number of different tribal names, such as the Gauls, the Galatians and the Celtiberians. These tribes were linked by certain linguistic, cultural and social traits.

The sources of Celtic art and design, typified by their intricate interlacing, knotwork and spiral patterns, are equally diffuse. For some, the first hints of the style can be detected in the later phases of the Hallstatt culture. This takes its name from a large cemetery in Austria, containing over 2000 graves, with the relevant 'Celtic' finds dating from the early Iron Age (Hallstatt 'C' and 'D' periods, c.700-500 BC). For most authorities, however, the Celtic achievement is associated much more closely with the La Tène culture which superseded it.

Like Hallstatt, La Tène was named after an archaeological type site located, in this instance, at the eastern end of Lake Neuchâtel in Switzerland. Opinions are divided as to the true nature of this settlement, but it seems likely that many of the objects deposited there were originally intended as sacrificial offerings, suggesting that it was a sacred place.

Since La Tène describes an unwieldy period that spans several centuries, historians usually divide it into four separate headings. These divisions – 'Early Style', 'Waldalgesheim Style', 'Plastic Style' and 'Sword Style' – offer useful guidelines, although the stages overlap chronologically and display considerable regional variation. Broadly speaking, however, 'Early Style' (emerging after c.480 BC) relates to the period of the great Celtic expansion and the assimilation of motifs from both the Classical world and the Orient. 'Waldalgesheim' (fl. after c.350 BC) owes its name to a princely chariot-grave discovered near Bonn and signals the growing maturity of the style. This is expressed most forcibly in the flowing, tendril-like patterns that adorn much of the jewellery of the period. During the 'Plastic' stage (fl. after c.290 BC), craftsmen paid greater attention to the three-dimensional qualities of human and animal forms, while the 'Sword Style' (fl. after c.190 BC) marked a return to designs that were flat, linear and abstract.

Viewed as a whole, the La Tène style was a cocktail of imported motifs – the lyre-scroll, the palmette, the Classical fret pattern, the lotus bud – blended skilfully with the geometric tendencies that were inherited from the Hallstatt culture. Significantly though, none of these individual elements were as important as the spirit of invention that bound them together. The strength of Celtic design lies in the dynamic interplay it provides between

Above: Detail from the Lindisfarne Gospels.

Facing page: The intricate opening letters of St Matthew's Gospel in The Durham Book, seventh century.

Above: Elaborate letters from the Book of Kells make creative use of animal forms.

Facing page: The beautifully illuminated opening page of St John's Gospel in the Lindisfarne Gospels.

sinuous, decorative forms. La Tène craftsmen steered a careful path between the extremes of geometric abstraction and sterile naturalism, avoiding the rigidity and repetition of the former and the purely imitative qualities of the latter. Instead, they employed a limited range of motifs – mostly spirals, knotwork, interlacing and diagonal key patterns – but varied these with such exuberance that the results are never monotonous. Often, they have the addictive appeal of a visual puzzle, tempting the viewer to look at an object again and again, mentally unravelling its design.

Human and animal figures were also featured, but usually in a highly stylized form. Legs, ears and tails taper away into strands of interlacing and the creatures themselves melt into abstract patterns. Conversely, simple geometric shapes, such as a pair of adjacent spirals, might be used to suggest eyes and horns, when looked at from a certain angle. Because of their elusive character, these have been dubbed 'Cheshire cat' designs, after the disappearing cat in *Alice's Adventures in Wonderland*. La Tène craftsmen were particularly fond of this teasing kind of pictorial ambiguity, a reflection, it seems, of their interest in metamorphosis. The Celtic pantheon included many deities that could shape-shift at will into birds and animals.

Despite this, suprisingly little about the beliefs of the Celts can be learned from their artworks. It is clear, however, that the severed human head was a potent symbol for them and that their warriors were feared as head-hunters. Evidence for this has been found among the remains of two hilltop shrines from ancient Gaul, at Entremont and Roquepertuse, where carved heads and human skulls were displayed side by side, either as trophies or offerings.

The Celts also had a particular reverence for water, regarding it as the dwelling place of healing and protective spirits. This is clearly indicated by the substantial number of rich artefacts that appear to have been deliberately deposited in rivers, lakes, marshes and springs. At La Tène, for example, special wooden platforms were erected, so that supplicants could cast their gifts into the deepest and most inaccessible parts of the lake. Similarly, at a shrine devoted to Sequana, the goddess of the River Seine, ailing pilgrims threw small wooden effigies of their diseased organs into the sacred pool, hoping that the river spirit would effect a cure for them. Along with the grave-goods excavated from their burial places, these sacrificical offerings have provided the best source of information about early Celtic art.

Nevertheless, representations of specific deities and their accompanying legends are frustratingly rare. One of the few exceptions to this rule is supplied by the imagery on the Gundestrup Cauldron which dates from about the first century BC. This cult vessel was discovered in a Danish peat bog, where it had apparently been left as a votive offering. On it, there are a series of narrative scenes, presumably illustrating incidents from the Celtic mythological canon. One of the figures, sitting cross-legged and wearing a set of antlers (page 117), is usually thought to represent

Above: The Symbols of the Evangelists adapted from the page which introduces St Mark's Gospel in the Book of Kells.

Facing page: Pages from the Book of Mac Durnan, ninth century, show (top) the 'Monogram Page' and (bottom) St John.

Cernunnos, the horned god of nature and fertility. Such is the scarcity of this type of image, however, that the interpretation of the remaining scenes can only be highly speculative.

Ironically, this general lack of narrative content prolonged the life of Celtic design considerably. For, in the fullness of time, Christian artists were able to borrow the swirling, curvilinear patterns they found on La Tène artefacts and use them as decoration in their Gospel Books or on their liturgical vessels. The ornamental virtues of the style enabled them to overlook its pagan origins.

By the time this process had begun, the focal point of Celtic creativity had shifted westwards. The growth of the Roman Empire had gradually subdued the original strongholds of La Tène culture in central and eastern Europe, replacing this with a provincial form of classicism. But the Roman legions did not conquer the entire continent. In Ireland and Scotland, for example, the La Tène tradition survived intact, even though it had reached these areas comparatively late.

Christianity arrived in England during the Roman occupation, but the systematic conversion of the British Isles began later and took place on two distinct fronts. Official papal missions were despatched by Celestine I, who appointed the first bishop of Ireland in 431, and by Gregory the Great, who organised the more celebrated expedition of St Augustine in 596. If the conversion had been achieved by these missions alone, using manuscripts and ecclesiastical equipment imported from Rome, then the history of later Celtic art might have been very different.

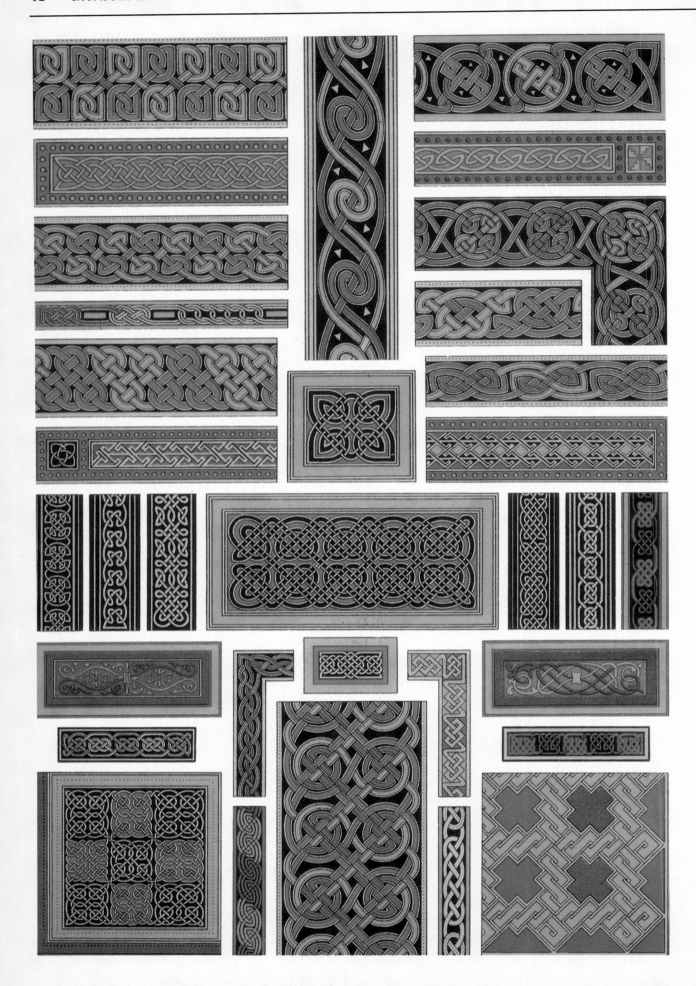

In fact, however, these efforts were matched by the teachings of St Patrick, St Columba and St Aidan. They did not operate within the framework of the Roman church, with its hierarchical emphasis on the diocesan system. Instead, they followed the ascetic monastic tradition that had developed in North Africa. Accordingly, the structure of their 'Celtic' Church was based around a network of monastic houses that were independent from Rome. The most important of these foundations were in Ireland and Northumbria, at places such as Durrow, Lindisfarne, Clonmacnois and Kells. In due course, each of these communities set up their own scriptorium, a workshop where manuscripts were created and copied.

The comparative independence of these centres ensured that the artworks produced by them or for their use were heavily influenced by native craftsmen working in the old La Tène tradition. The most celebrated of these items are the illuminated Gospel Books, which some regard as the supreme achievements of Celtic design. Thus, in the Book of Durrow (c.675), we can find extravagant spiral motifs that have direct parallels with those adorning prehistoric weaponry and armour while, in the Book of Kells (c.800), there are intricate zoomorphic (animal-based) features that echo the decoration on the finest La Tène jewellery.

The Celtic Church eventually agreed to accept the full authority of the Papacy at the Synod of Whitby (664). By this stage, the monastic scriptoria were already established and Rome began sending manuscripts to be copied there. This accounts for the hybrid nature of many of the Gospel Books. In general terms, the Continental elements are most evident in the Biblical scenes and the depictions of the apostles, while the Celtic influence is strongest in the ornamental 'Carpet-pages' and in the sections devoted to calligraphy. In any event, the outstanding workmanship of these Insular manuscripts (i.e. British and Irish, as opposed to Continental) was fully appreciated. With a satisfying symmetry, many of them were exported to mainland Europe, to assist with the conversion of the old Celtic heartlands.

Manuscripts were not the only artworks created in the Christian era. A wide variety of shrines and liturgical vessels were also produced, boasting the same rich decoration that had featured on La Tène metalwork. Unfortunately, these precious objects proved a tempting prize for the Viking pillagers, who began their raids at the end of the eighth century. Lindisfarne and Iona were sacked, as were many of the Irish communities, and scores of these treasures were lost. Some of this loot has resurfaced in Scandinavia since the nineteenth century while, in Ireland, other pieces were buried for safe-keeping by frightened clerics and have since been excavated. The two most important hoards to be preserved in this way were unearthed at Derrynaflan in 1980 and Ardagh in 1868.

Celtic crosses also date from this period. Often, they were erected in monastic precincts where it was hoped they might provide some spiritual protection against the heathen desecrations. More realistically, they served as gathering places for outdoor prayers or as memorials for local saints. For obvious reasons, these crosses weathered the Viking storm more success-

Previous pages: Ornamentation taken from various Gospel Books, seventh to ninth centuries. Page 12: Examples of knotwork, interlacing and key patterns and a rudimentary swastika (second from top, right). Page 13: Interlacing and animal patterns.

Above: Dragon-like motif from the Book of Mac Durnan.

Facing page: Decorative borders and letters from The Durham Book.

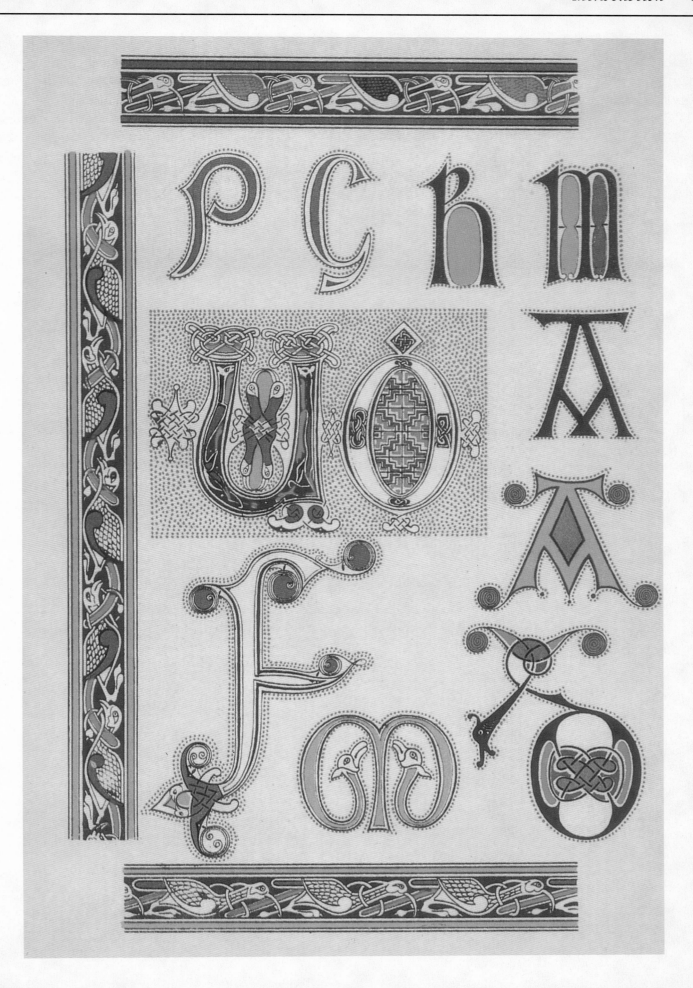

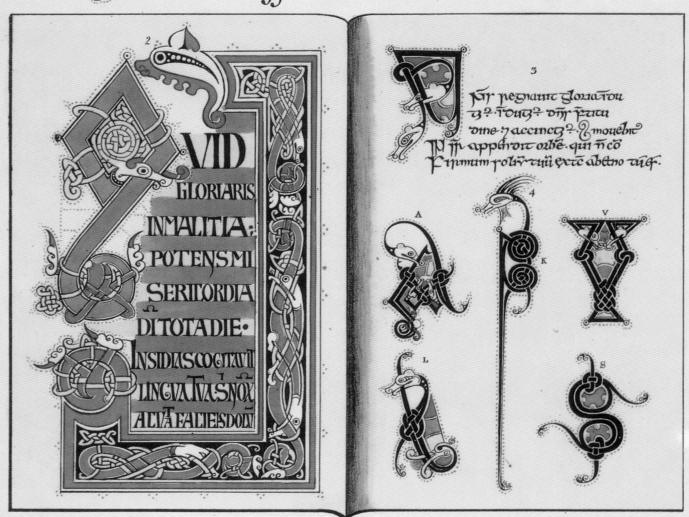

*Psalter of Ricemarchus &c.*

fully than the portable assets of the monks. In common with other church artefacts, however, they began to lose their Celtic character once the invaders started to settle in the area and be converted to Christianity. Accordingly, a succession of Scandinavian styles such as Jellinge, Mammen and Ringerike can be detected in the final phases of Celtic metalwork and stonework.

The Viking and Norman incursions eventually engulfed the last outposts of the La Tène tradition and the final traces of its influence were absorbed into the developing Romanesque style. In the centuries that followed, there were periodic revivals of interest in the Celts, although these were focused around literary themes – the Arthurian cycle of legends and the highly-romanticised theories about the Druids. The few artefacts that had come to light were not highly regarded, since they lacked the naturalism that has been the mainstay of Western art since the Renaissance.

The most significant of these revivals was sparked off by the discovery of the Tara Brooch in 1850. This came into the possession of George Waterhouse, a Dublin jeweller, who marketed reproductions of the article. The success of his venture was guaranteed when Queen Victoria purchased two copies of the brooch at the Great Exhibition of 1851, thereby creating a fashion. For the first time, Celtic designs were imitated or reinterpreted on a large scale. This trend reached a peak at the end of the century, when Liberty's of London introduced a full range of goods sporting a Celtic inter-lace pattern – among them, tea sets, candlesticks, clocks and cigarette cases.

One interesting sidelight on the Tara Brooch is that its name was an inven-tion. The original find had actually been made at Bettystown, but Waterhouse preferred to give it a romantic aura (in Irish lore, Tara was revered as the ancient seat of its kings). This formed part of a growing tendency for various nationalist movements – Irish, Scottish and Breton – to stress their Celtic inheritance as a vindication of their cause. This is ironic, as the original Celts were always a supra-national race.

In the twentieth century, the prestige of Celtic art has been greatly enhanced. In part, this is due to our increasing knowledge of the subject, but a great debt is also owed to the Modernist rejection of naturalism and the rediscovery of so-called 'primitive' cultures. It seems certain that future generations will continue to enjoy and experiment with the limitless intri-cacies of Celtic design.

This book has been designed for easy reference with designs divided into eight chapters – Interlacing and Knotwork, Spirals and Circles, Calligraphy, Geometric Designs, Figurative Designs, Jewellery, Artefacts and Stonework – covering the entire range of Celtic patterns and motifs. A brief commen-tary opens each chapter to explain the various techniques of Celtic art and design and informative captions highlight particular details.

Facing page: Graphic designs based on serpentine forms from the Psalter of Ricemarchus.

# Interlacing & Knotwork

Ultimately, interlace designs are derived from three-dimensional crafts, such as textile weaving and basketry. Unfortunately, the artworks produced in these media have not endured, making direct comparisons with surviving forms impossible. Instead, the most immediate sources of Celtic design are to be found in Roman pavements and Coptic manuscripts. These, in turn, can be traced back to Greek vases and artefacts from prehistoric Mesopotamia.

The simplest form of interlacing is plaitwork (examples of this can be seen to the right of page 47). This regular, repetitive design was useful for covering broad areas of stone or vellum, but the effect was monotonous. Greater variety was achieved by the introduction of 'breaks' in the plaiting. This enabled artists to experiment with smaller patterns of complex knots and also offered scope for secondary designs. These could be formed by the 'breaks' in the overall scheme and in Christian artworks, they usually took the form of a cross. Thus, for example, four distinct crosses can be discerned amid the plaiting on the shaft at Llantwit Major (page 177). This type of pattern was particularly popular with the Celts, as its subtleties were not immediately apparent. In this sense, it is an abstract variant of their 'Cheshire cat' designs (see introduction).

As their knotwork patterns became more elaborate, Celtic craftsmen began to create effects that no weaver or basket-maker could hope to emulate. This was because two-dimensional interlacing strands could be manipulated much more easily that the genuine materials that they were imitating. A ribbon could expand or taper away, as the design required. The introduction of angular lines opened up further possibilities. Pointed loops enabled artists to fill the corners of rectangular shapes, such as stonework panels or manuscript pages, much more satisfactorily. They also made internal designs more versatile. In the knotwork border at the top of page 24, for example, crosses were formed at the junctions of four pointed loops. Similarly, in the images at the centre of page 25, they were used to produce squares, crosses, triangles and lozenges.

In the Gospel Books, interlace patterns are most evident on the aptly-named Carpet-pages (page 24). These are purely ornamental, containing no text and no illustrations of biblical events, although they do normally feature a cross. Knotwork designs can also be found in the decorative panels of much Celtic stonework and they were sometimes fashioned into the shape of the cross itself (pages 46 and 47). It may seem strange in the twentieth century that a decorative motif could be used to convey a sacred emblem but, for the Celts, ornamentation carried no frivolous overtones. In a depiction of Adam and Eve (page 173), it was perfectly acceptable to incorporate the Serpent and the Tree of Knowledge into a knotwork pattern without undermining the sanctity of the scene.

The Celts loved to achieve a sense of visual trickery in their abstract designs. Several of these patterns, for example (top, far right), appear at first glance to be composed of interlocking circles. Closer examination reveals, however, that none of the rings is complete.

The simplest key border (this page, centre, right) is formed by two continuous, narrow bands, which cross over at regular intervals. More intriguing effects are achieved by using extra bands or by enclosing the crossing, as other examples on these pages reveal.

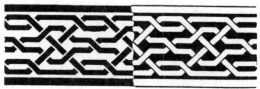

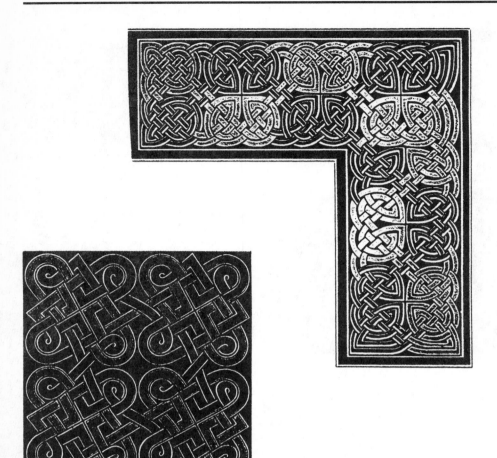

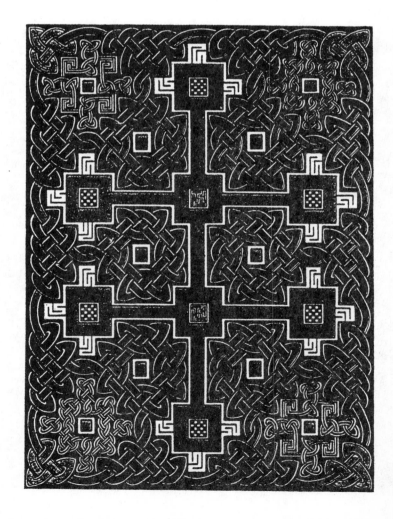

The large detail on this page (right) is the Cross carpet-page, which opens the Book of Durrow. The central motif is a double-barred cross. Four inter-laced crosses feature in the corners, and there are clockwise, key-pattern projections on six of the squares, creating a spiral effect.

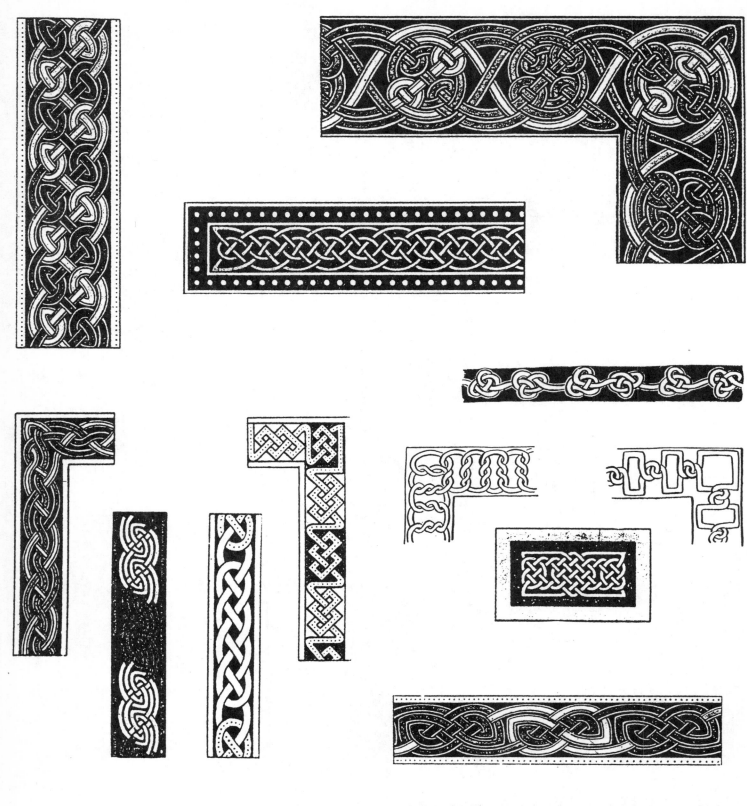

The use of a second colour brought an added dimension to manuscript decoration, as in these border designs taken mainly from the Gospel Books. Sometimes, it emphasized the true path of the thread (right); at others, it could be used to form artificial groupings (top, far right).

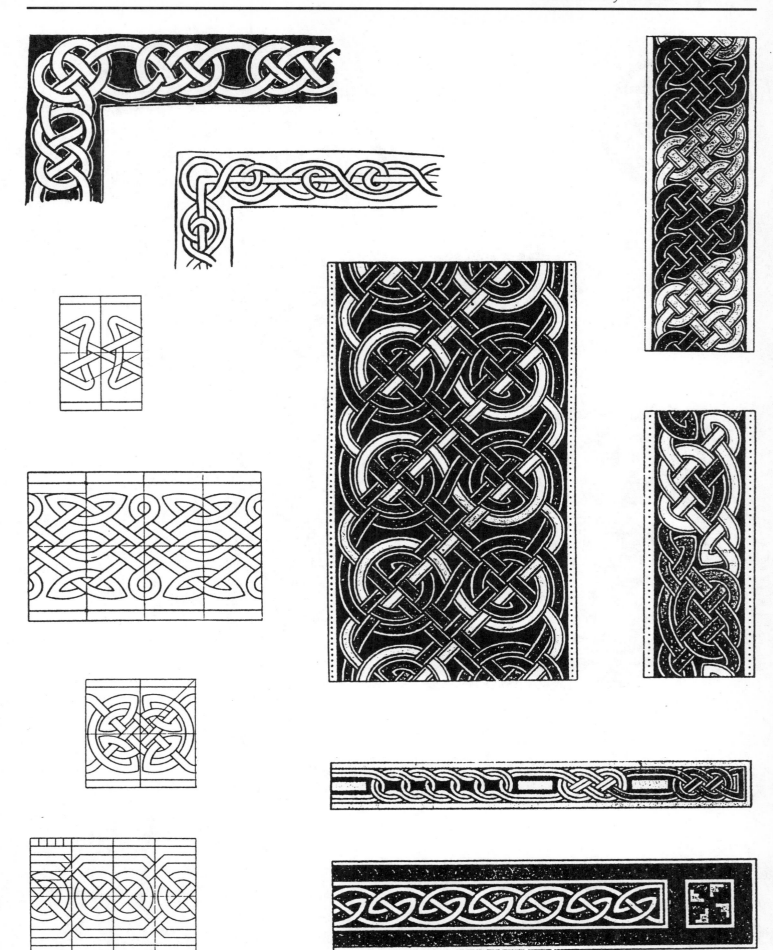

The constant search for new ways of evoking the image of the cross taxed the ingenuity of Christian artists. Some of their solutions are pictured in the smaller images on these pages. The use of the triquetra or Trinity symbol (this page, top, left and facing page, centre) was particularly effective.

Many of these examples are taken from stonework
in Scotland often forming part of larger designs.
The circular motif on the facing page (centre, right)
is half of the Pictish double disc or 'spectacles'
symbol. This version is from a cross-slab at St
Vigeans, Tayside.

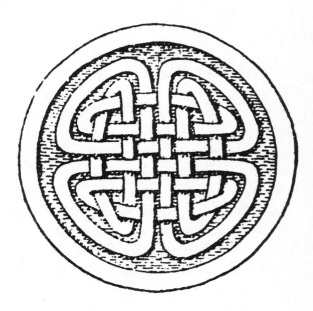

When designing borders, Celtic artists liked to emphasise corners by using pointed or 'fishtail' loops (facing page, top, left). Alternatively, the pattern could terminate abruptly in the base line of a triangle (facing page, top, right and bottom, centre).

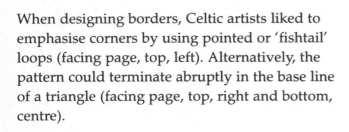

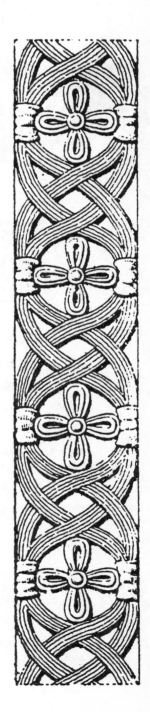

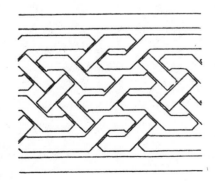

The four lower diagrams on the facing page illustrate the diagonal structure at the heart of many linked circle designs, including the design (centre, left), which is a multiple variant of the ring-chain motif.

In his seminal work of 1904, J. Romilly Allen, an early specialist in the field of Celtic art, identified eight basic knots, which he believed were at the root of most Celtic design. These are featured here along the top row, with some of their variants beneath.

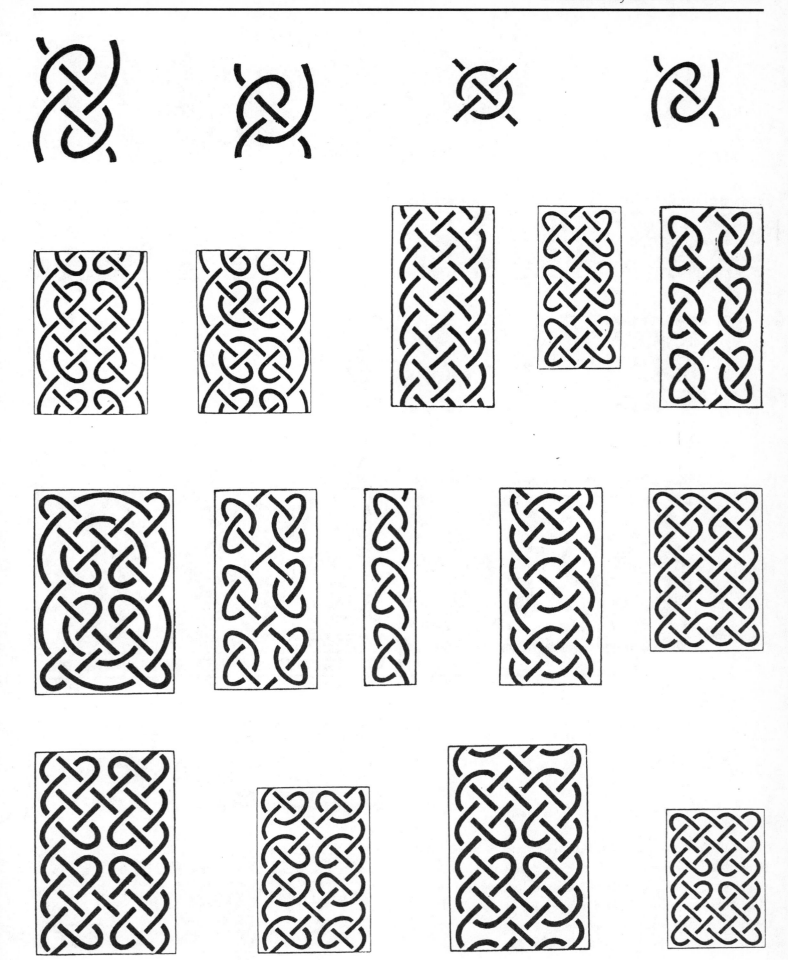

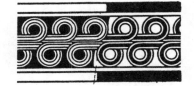

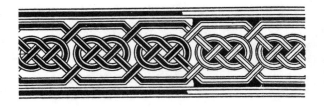

The two designs at the foot of the facing page illustrate how many knotwork borders can be built up from a square grid, with pointed loops at the four corners. In the design above, this structure is artfully masked by the row of circles which join adjacent grids, creating a new visual focus.

Even the most basic designs can form secondary patterns. Thus, a quartet of triangular knots (facing page, second from top) can suggest a St Andrew's Cross, and a simple series of loops (right) can resemble a Maltese Cross.

The small panel above is taken from a manuscript and is an admirable example of Celtic invention. Three separate motifs - spiral, key pattern and interlacing - are combined effortlessly in a very limited space.

The bifurcating plaitwork design (facing page, third from top) is a looser form of the ring-chain motif, which originated in Scandinavia and which is featured on much stonework in the north of England.

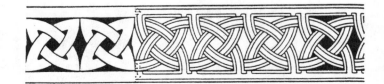

The complex interlace pattern on the Carndonagh
Cross, Co. Donegal (facing page, top, left), is based
around a structure of four elongated triangular
knots. Three birds nestle under each side of the bar,
forming a spiral with their beaks. This stone slab
was one of the first to be specially carved into the
shape of a cross.

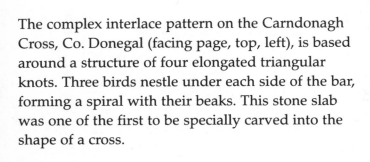

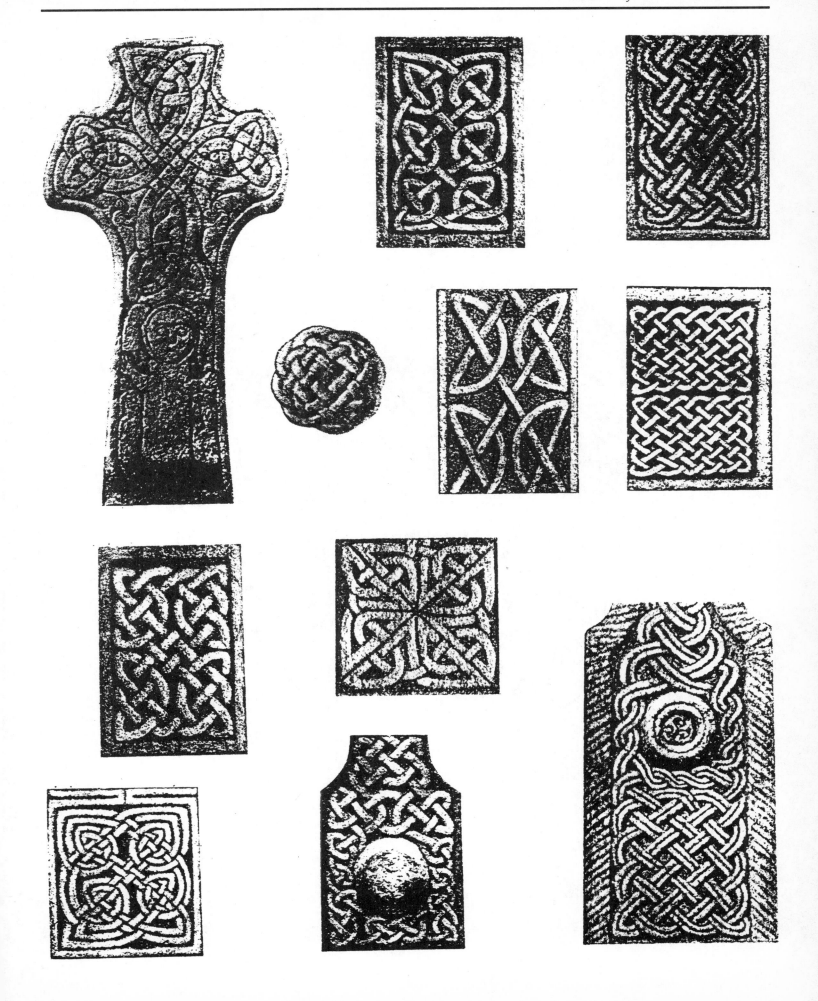

# Spirals & Circles

The use of the spiral motif pre-dated the La Tène era by many centuries, but its visible presence on the stone monuments left by previous generations may have provided a source of inspiration for the Celts. Spiral designs could be seen at the passage graves of Gavr'inis in Brittany and Newgrange in Ireland (page 56); on carved stone balls, such as the one found at Towrie in northern Scotland (page 56); and on the Neolithic cup-and-ring marks, sculpted into rocks in many isolated regions (page 55).

There appears to have been a symbolic purpose behind some of these spiral patterns. At Gavr'inis, the absence of human remains has given rise to suggestions that the place was as much a ritual centre as a tomb. This, added to the fact that both Gavr'inis and Newgrange were carefully aligned with the winter sunrise, has fuelled the theory that the spirals may have been solar symbols. Certainly, this was true of the swastika, a variant of the spiral motif which was much favoured by Celtic artists. In both cases, the rotating lines have been interpreted as a representation of the sun's movement across the sky.

In terms of design, the La Tène craftsmen made great advances on these earlier models. The patterns on the Towrie and Newgrange carvings, for example, are based on simple, one-coil spirals. The Celtic versions are generally more elaborate. Usually, they radiate out from a centre of three or four lines, forming a triskele or a swastika at the heart of the spiral (the triskele is a three-legged motif, best-known from the Isle of Man's emblem). Sometimes, the central image is even more complex. It may be composed of a triangle within a circle (page 51) or a knotwork pattern (bottom of page 52).

The Celts also brought new refinements to the arrangement of spiral groupings. At Newgrange, there were spirals linked together as triangles (bottom of page 58) and these were later echoed in some manuscript designs (page 53). More often, though, La Tène artists used S or C-shapes to link their spirals. The C-shape is closely related to the pelta motif, which has been likened to the cross-section of a mushroom with a curling cap. Several examples of this can be seen on page 50, including a complex, interlocking design where spirals are shared between adjacent peltas.

The key feature of Celtic spiral patterns was balance. Invariably, the two curves of S and C-shapes were filled with spirals rotating in opposite directions. This same principle also applied when more spirals were involved. On several of the images on page 51, for instance, three spirals orbit around a fourth one at the centre. They are linked by long, tapering curves known as 'trumpet spirals'. In each case, the fact that the central motif is rotating in the opposite direction to its satellites helps to introduce a note of calm and stillness at the core of the swirling composition.

A selection of spiral designs from Celtic stonework and manuscripts. Many achieve a sense of balance by contrasting clockwise and anti-clockwise spirals. Others are structured around the basic C-curve or pelta shape, such as the semicircular carving from a slab at Clonfert, Co. Galway (this page, bottom, right).

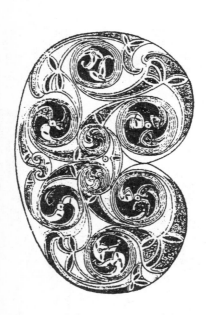

Celtic artists have sometimes been accused of a 'horror vacui' - a compulsive desire to decorate every available space. In the 'O' from the Lindisfarne Gospels (this page, top, right) the central void is more ornate than the letter itself. Equally elaborate is the void within the letter 'Q' (above).

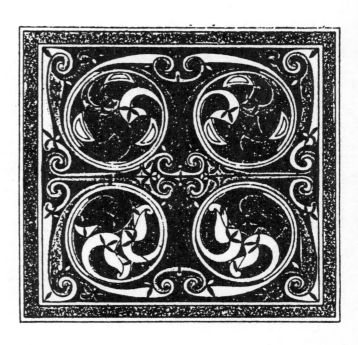

Zoomorphic elements added an extra dimension to spiral decoration. The playful design (top, right) invites the viewer to link the birds' heads with their shared claws. The delicately engraved pattern (top, left) comes from a gold torc found at Broighter, Co. Derry.

Cup-and-ring marks from Co. Donegal. The
purpose of these enigmatic rock carvings is hotly
disputed, but the most popular theories suggest
that they had some astronomical significance and
were perhaps related to a solar cult.

Spirals and circles on stone carvings from Towie,
Grampian (right), and Newgrange, Co. Meath
(above right). They decorate three bronze scabbards
from Lisnacroghera, Co. Antrim (bottom, far right),
and to their left, an enamelled bowl handle.

A swastika is a spiral shape made with straight lines. The curious rock carving at Ilkley, W. Yorkshire (this page, top, right) falls somewhere between the two. The more traditional, angular form of the swastika can be seen in the design at the top of the facing page. This is based on the central boss of the Battersea shield, British Museum.

Celtic mirrors are noted for their finely-engraved backs. The example from Birdlip, Gloucestershire (top, left) displays a natural, flowing rhythm. By contrast, the stonework designs on the facing page are much more symmetrical. The finest of these is from Kinnitty Cross, Co. Offaly (far right), where six coils radiate from a large, central spiral.

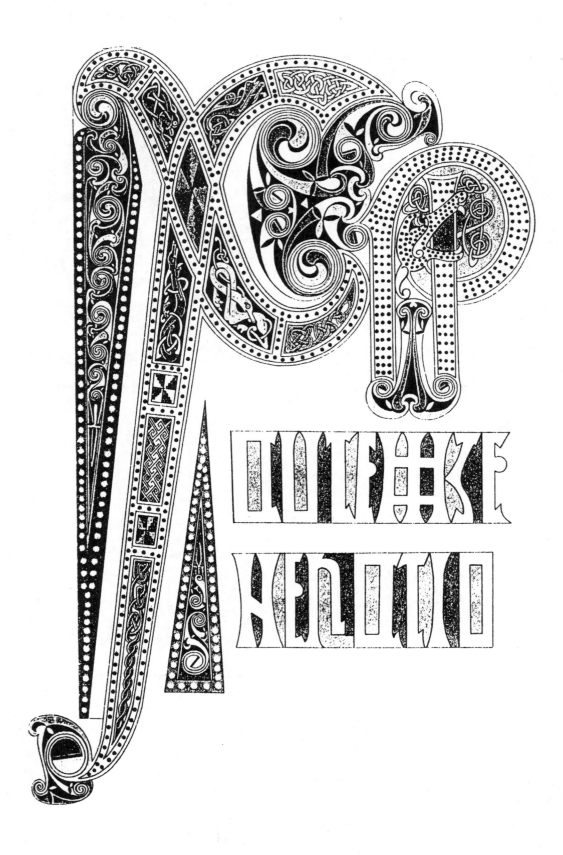

# Calligraphy

Prior to the arrival of Christianity, the western Celts had no established form of written language. In Ireland, the nearest equivalent was Ogham, an extremely primitive type of script, which has only survived through a number of carved inscriptions.

Early missionaries placed a mystical emphasis on the written word and this was reflected in the calligraphy of Celtic manuscripts. There were huge initial letters, which filled the length of a page; there were complex combinations of characters that were barely decipherable; and the words themselves could be broken up arbitrarily to fit the overall design of the page. In short, the most ornate of the Gospel Books were like magical talismans, revealing their treasures only to the initiated.

The actual script was derived from a Classical source. Irish scribes used an elegant form of lettering based on the distinctively rounded characters of Roman half-uncial script. The curves of the letters were accentuated in the Gospels as, unlike their continental counterparts, Insular (British and Irish) calligraphers made little use of compasses, preferring to draw freehand.

It is the ornamental nature of Celtic manuscripts, however, that has secured their reputation. The simplest form of decoration was a series of red dots, following the contours of individual letters and lending them an impression of depth  (page 86). The characters themselves were also decorated, initially with colour alone but later, with interlace and knotwork patterns.

In the Book of Durrow, the ornamentation was entirely abstract. Plaitwork and interlacing filled the internal structure of the letters, while elaborate spirals unfurled at every terminal (examples on pages 68 and 69). By the time that the Lindisfarne Gospels were produced, zoomorphic motifs were more common. Writhing bird and animal shapes formed interlace designs in and between the characters, and heads emerged as spirals at the terminals. Some of the calligraphic combinations were also highly decorative. The image created by the opening letters of 'Mattheus' (page 65), for example, bears a charming resemblance to the clasp of a brooch.

The analogy with jewellery is even more striking in the Book of Kells. Here, the decoration within individual letters was often split into several segments, rather like cloisonné panels. In this sense, it is interesting to compare the 'L' and the 'N' on pages 82 and 83 with the intricate compartments on the Tara brooch (pages 140 and 141). Zoomorphic motifs, too, were much more elaborate. While, in many Continental manuscripts, animals were passively manipulated into the shapes of letters (pages 84 and 85), some characters in the Book of Kells resembled miniature battlegrounds. An 'A' (page 65), for example, was represented by the wrestling figures of a man, a bird and a beast, whose bitter conflict distorted the letter so much that it was barely identifiable.

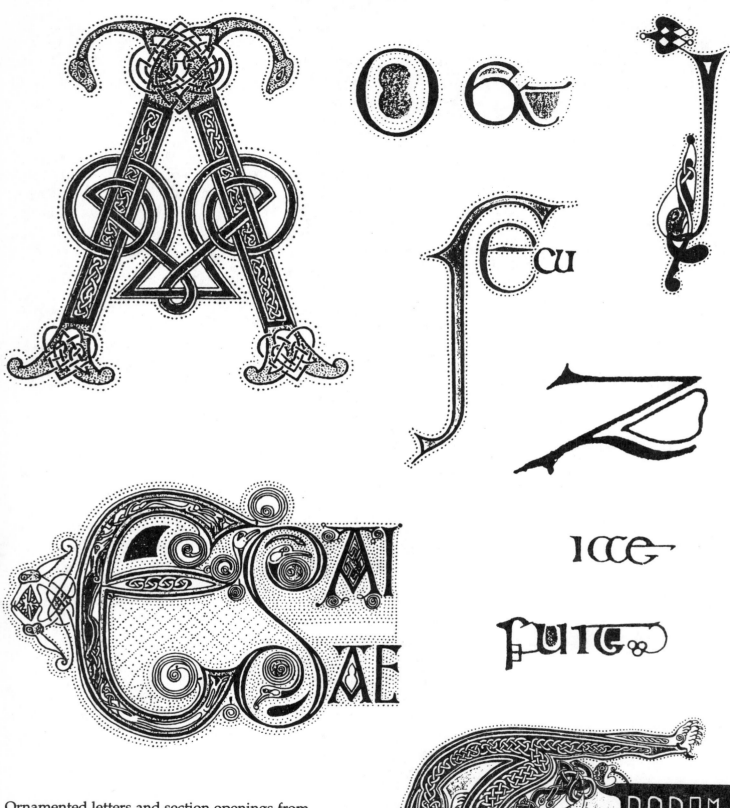

Ornamented letters and section openings from
the Gospel Books. The ferocious, leonine creature
which forms the 'T' of 'Tunc' (right) comes from
the 'Crucifixion page' in the Book of Kells.
A similar sense of refinement can also be found
in 'Mattheus' (top, far right) and 'Esaiae' (above),
from the Lindisfarne manuscript.

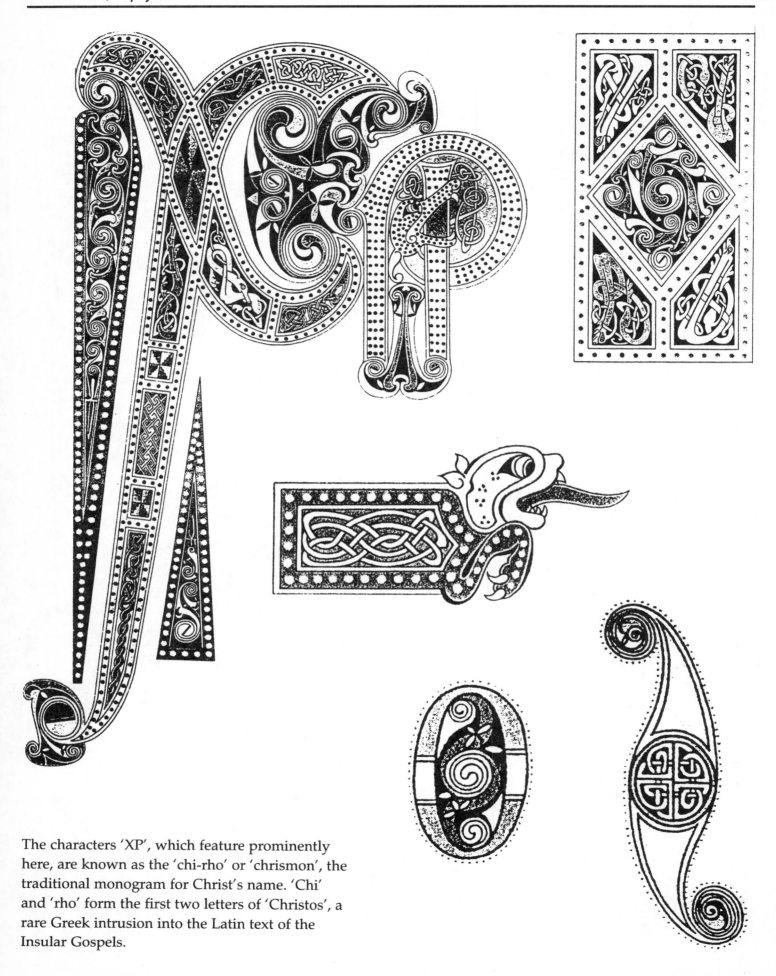

The characters 'XP', which feature prominently
here, are known as the 'chi-rho' or 'chrismon', the
traditional monogram for Christ's name. 'Chi'
and 'rho' form the first two letters of 'Christos', a
rare Greek intrusion into the Latin text of the
Insular Gospels.

The Book of Kells features some extraordinary
ligatures of two or more letters. The combination
above represents 'CA'; the interwoven dog and
serpent (centre, right) form 'DI'; while the motif
with the fish (facing page, centre) denotes 'TU'.
The 'F' and 'Q' (top, far left and right) are
fine examples of the spiral decoration in the
Book of Durrow.

Angular script from the Book of Kells (above and right) displays several variations of each character, together with letters from an eighth-century Galician manuscript (top, right). Zoomorphic initials cover the facing page.

The taste for elaborate spiral and interlace designs proved an enduring one. The examples on the facing page derive from a bible owned by Louis le Débonnaire, the son and heir of Charlemagne. The images on this page are taken from tenth-century French manuscripts.

Highly decorative letters from British, Irish and Continental manuscripts.

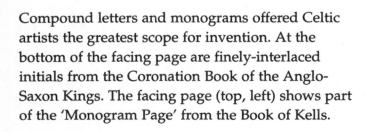

Compound letters and monograms offered Celtic artists the greatest scope for invention. At the bottom of the facing page are finely-interlaced initials from the Coronation Book of the Anglo-Saxon Kings. The facing page (top, left) shows part of the 'Monogram Page' from the Book of Kells.

The larger letters (far left and right) come from a
ninth-century Latin Bible. Between them, there are
a variety of characters from Continental manuscripts of the preceding century. Note how the
elongated fish tail transforms an 'O' into a 'Q'.

Sometimes animals were formed into the shape of individual letters, such as the pair of fish on the facing page. Celtic artists also combined them more subtly with abstract motifs. The six fish (top, right) for example, contain triangular knots, which echo the larger triquetras in the design.

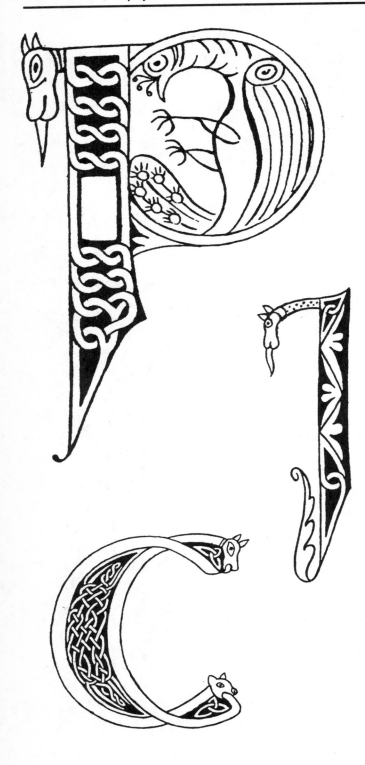

The full repertoire of Celtic motifs is amply demonstrated here. The 'N' and the 'L' (facing page top, left and this page, right) both come from the Book of Kells and feature animal interlacing, spirals and key patterns. The 'O' from the Lindisfarne Gospels (facing page) is equally magnificent.

A selection of zoomorphic designs from
eighth-century Continental manuscripts.

These characters are from a seventh-century Anglo-Saxon psalter. The use of red dots around the contours of the letters is one of the simplest forms of Celtic decoration and has parallels in Coptic manuscripts. The contrasting spiral orna-mentation has affinities with the Book of Durrow.

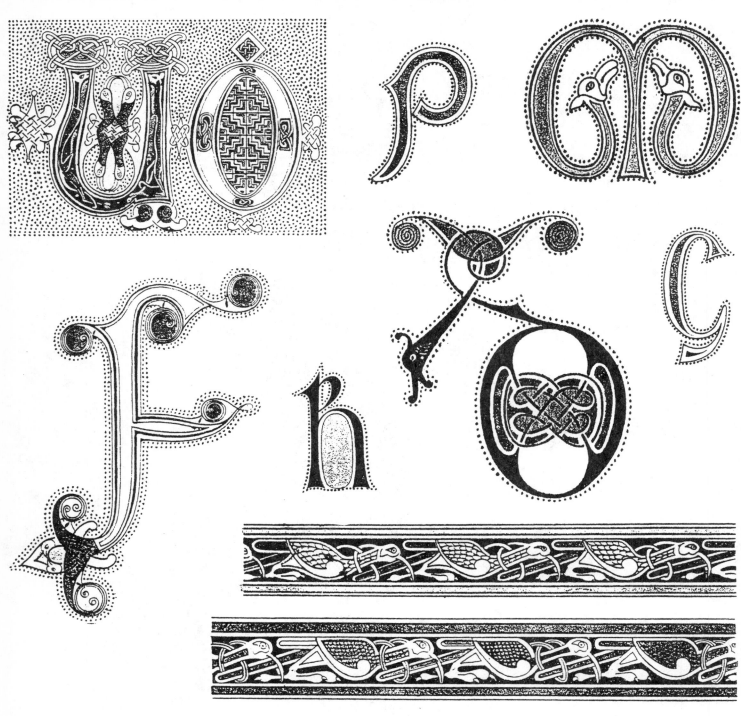

Above: examples of interlaced letters and birds
from the Durham Gospels - a manuscript that has
strong stylistic links with the Lindisfarne Gospels.
On the facing page: samples of characters from
eighth-century Continental texts.

# Geometric Designs

For many people, the Celtic style is so epitomized by the curvilinear forms of spirals, knots and interlacing that its geometric elements can be overlooked. Rectilinear shapes did play an important part in Celtic design, however, particularly during the Christian era, when they featured strongly on stonework and in manuscript decoration.

The dominant rectilinear motifs were the Greek key or fret patterns (pages 92 and 105). These are most closely associated with the Classical world, although there is some disagreement as to whether the Celts borrowed them directly from this source. In any event, they deployed them very differently. Classical key patterns were used principally in horizontal or vertical bands. This is rare in Celtic art, although examples can be found, on Penmon Cross (page 186), and at the bottom of some cross-shafts (e.g. page 177, left).

Instead, the Celts preferred to employ diagonal key patterns and did not restrict their use to border decoration. This enabled them to create attractive, overlapping designs, such as the one at Aberlady (page 99), where the fret motifs resemble straight-line spirals. The disadvantage of this approach, however, was that it left blank, undecorated areas at the edge of the panel. Stonemasons solved this problem by reducing the size of the line and by adding extra 45 degree turns. The other designs on page 98 illustrate the compressed, maze-like images that could be created in this way.

Step patterns achieved a similar effect. As the name suggests, these resembled a flight of stairs and a typical example can be seen within the lozenge on page 93. At first glance, this may seem to be composed of symmetrical triangles but, as so often with Celtic art, appearances can be deceptive. The design is actually formed out of a single, continuous line.

In many ways, the Celtic treatment of angular shapes was very close to its use of spiral and interlace motifs. This is most evident from the general enthusiasm for creating secondary patterns within the overall design. Diagonal crosses and swastikas were particularly popular motifs. The latter were sometimes formed by interlocking T-shapes (page 100, top, left) and sometimes by diagonal key patterns (page 176, left).

Square and chequer patterns were also used in Celtic art, although examples of these are quite scarce. In most instances, they can be found as enamel inlays on metal artefacts, where they provide striking contrasts with the surrounding curvilinear design. The armlet from Castle Newe (page 130) offers a good example. This effect was mimicked in some manuscripts as well (e.g. page 24, bottom), demonstrating the close links between different Celtic art forms.

Celtic key patterns have strong affinities with the classical Greek fret motif (this page, centre). Traditionally, however, their format is diagonal rather than horizontal and the interlocking sections are more tightly packed. The step design (facing page, centre) was also much favoured by Celtic artists.

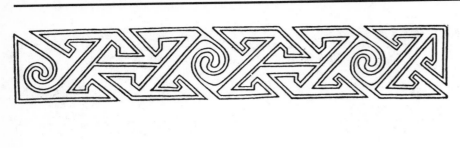

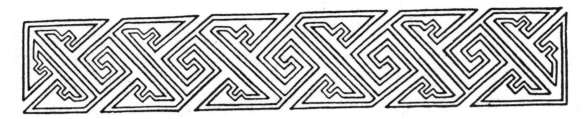

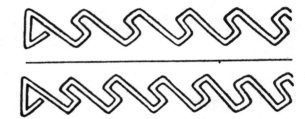

A selection of fret patterns from Irish stonework. Semicircular designs often form part of the crosses on memorial slabs. On the facing page (top, centre), there is one of a matching pair from Suibne's grave at Clonmacnois, Co. Offaly. These are on the lateral arms, with the straight edge facing outwards, so that the arrow-head motif complements the horizontal bar.

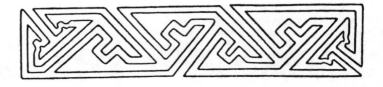

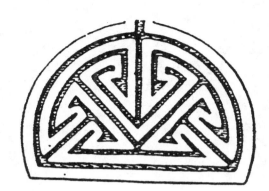

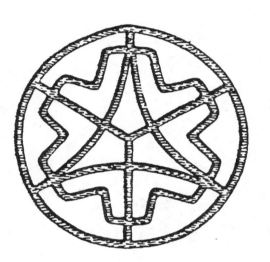

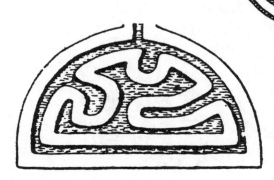
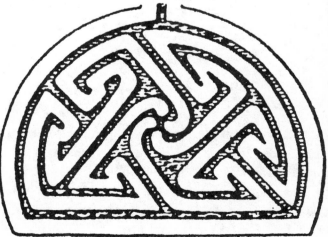

A variety of triangles, swastikas and crosses from
Celtic stonework, which were often rendered as
forms of interlacing. The terminals of one of the
crosses (facing page, top, left) contains triquetras
or triangular knots; this is highly appropriate, since
triquetras symbolize the Trinity.

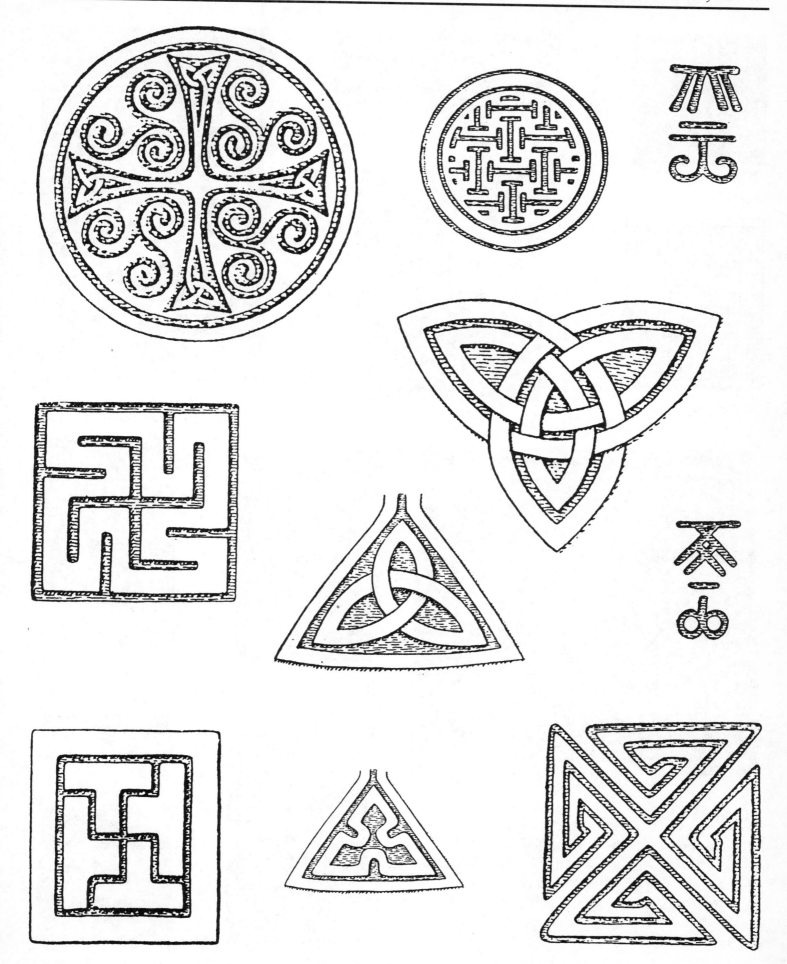

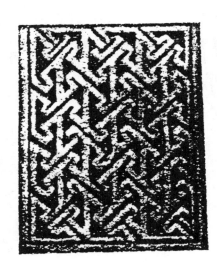

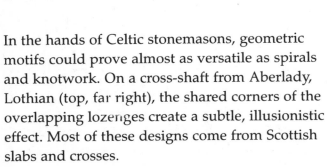

In the hands of Celtic stonemasons, geometric motifs could prove almost as versatile as spirals and knotwork. On a cross-shaft from Aberlady, Lothian (top, far right), the shared corners of the overlapping lozenges create a subtle, illusionistic effect. Most of these designs come from Scottish slabs and crosses.

There was considerable cross-fertilization between different Celtic art forms. The design of the Pictish slab at Rosemarkie, Highland (bottom, far right), bears a striking resemblance to some of the cross-pages in the Gospel manuscripts.

A selection of border patterns featuring interlocking lozenges, chevrons and floral motifs.

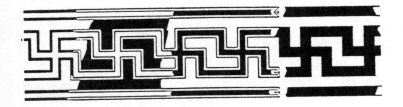

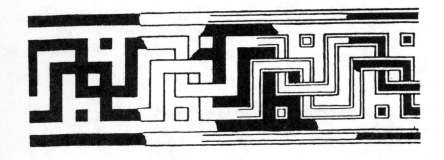

A selection of border patterns. Several feature
swastikas, a symbol that represented the sun and
was common to many cultures. The design at the
top (left) incorporates an angular version of the
pelta motif. The fret pattern (facing page, centre,
left) was essentially a Classical form, although it
does appear on Celtic stonework.

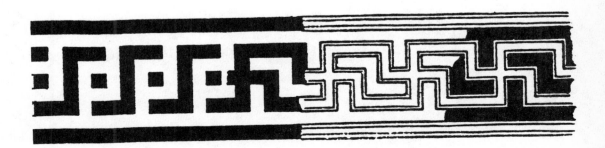

# Figurative Designs

Figurative elements featured prominently in Celtic art and can be found on artefacts and jewellery from the earliest La Tène era. Later on, their continuing popularity with Christian artists culminated in the marvellous, zoomorphic inventions in the Book of Kells.

The treatment of these motifs varied considerably. When they were in a narrative context, there was obviously a degree of naturalism. This is most evident in the portraits of the Evangelists in the Gospel Books and in the biblical scenes on some Celtic crosses. Other, less convincing claims suggest that some of the birds in the Lindisfarne Gospels resemble the cormorants and shags that could have been seen nesting near the monastery.

Elsewhere in Celtic manuscripts, creatures could be symbolic. The emblems of the Evangelists – which included an eagle, an ox and a lion – are instantly recognizable. Many, however, are less clear. One of the earliest Christian symbols, for example, was the fish and a reference to this may be intended by the curious creature in the Book of Kells, which is part-man, part-fish (page 115). In addition, the frequent depiction of reptiles on La Tène artworks is often seen as a reflection of pagan serpent worship – the Celts revered snakes as emblems of fertility and healing. It has been suggested that, even in the Christian manuscripts, they were included as apotropaic symbols, designed to ward off evil.

In the majority of cases, though, figurative elements were used purely as ornamental motifs. Humans appeared mainly as wrestlers or beard-tuggers, but their actions were less important than the patterns they formed with their limbs. These might consist of swastikas, knots or plaitwork (page 118). Zoomorphic figures proved even more versatile and fell into three general categories – birds, reptiles and quadrupeds. The latter usually resembled dogs, lions or, very occasionally, cattle. The treatment of these was rarely anatomically correct. Certain features might be identifiable – a head, a haunch, a claw – but the rest of the 'body' was transformed into abstract ribbons, ready to participate in the most extravagant interlace patterns.

The fact that these motifs were ornamental did not necessarily mean that they were cheerful. There is an element of gallows humour in some designs, where men and birds tie themselves up in knots (page 114) or where an animal ends up biting its own paw. Often there are more savage undercurrents, as in the circular design where three dogs pursue each other with an air of desperation, each gripping the tail of the one in front (page 113). Scenes like this appear in the Gospels, irrespective of their context. One of the most vicious images, for example, depicts an animal's snout clamped firmly in the fangs of a second beast (page 115, top, right). Yet both this and the portrayal of a man suffering a similar fate (page 115) are featured on the opening page of St Luke's Gospel – an eloquent reminder of the heathen origins of later Celtic art.

The figurative elements on Celtic crosses are extremely diverse. Many portray biblical scenes. The panel to the right depicts Adam and Eve and the murder of Abel. Others are more enigmatic, such as the crouching figure (facing page, centre, left), which is thought to represent a pagan burial.

Most of these interlocking birds and reptiles come from the Book of Kells, but this type of design was equally popular with sculptors. The four hair and beard-pulling figures (facing page, top, left) come from a cross-shaft at Clonmacnois.

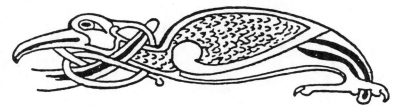

Most of the creatures in Celtic manuscripts were highly fanciful. When they served a symbolic purpose, however, they were much more recognizable. The eagle (above, right) was an emblem of St John while the peacock (facing page, centre, right) was a symbol of the Resurrection.

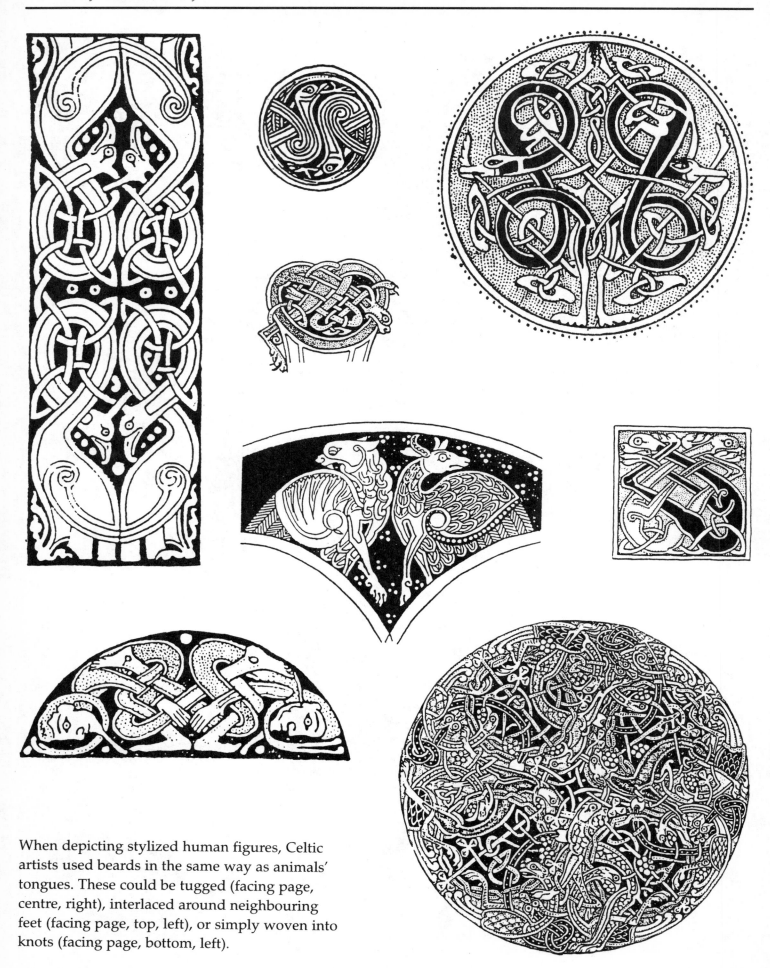

When depicting stylized human figures, Celtic artists used beards in the same way as animals' tongues. These could be tugged (facing page, centre, right), interlaced around neighbouring feet (facing page, top, left), or simply woven into knots (facing page, bottom, left).

The treatment of the human form during the pagan era was very different from that of the Christian age that followed it. The cross-legged figure on the facing page comes from the Gundestrup cauldron. He is thought to represent a Celtic deity, possibly the horned god, Cernunnos.

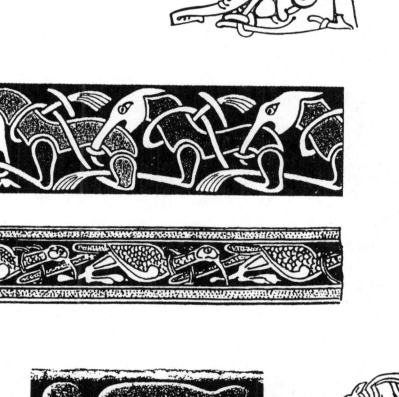

Zoomorphic elements could be adapted to form any geometric shape. The legs of the hair-pulling children from the cross at Old Kilcullen, Co. Kildare (above) create the outline of a swastika, while below this the serpentine body of a two-headed creature forms a reversible key pattern.

# Jewellery

For the Celts, the most important form of personal adornment was the torc. This heavy metal collar was of eastern origin and findings from the early La Tène period are more common to female graves. Later it was worn by both sexes and was regarded as a token of rank or divinity. Classical writers noted that Boudicca wore a golden neckring into battle and one of the largest collections of torcs (the Snettisham hoard) was discovered in the area of eastern England over which she ruled. Similarly, Celtic artists usually depicted their deities with torcs. On the Gundestrup cauldron, for example, the god Cernunnos is shown wearing one and holding up a second (page 117).

The decoration on torcs could be quite elaborate and was usually focused on the terminals. Sometimes the patterns were abstract, as on the Clevedon fragments (page 128), but Celtic craftsmen were particularly fond of using human or animal heads (page 129), so that they could confront each other at the wearer's throat.

Anklets and armrings were in production throughout the La Tène era, but the finest examples were made in the 'Plastic Style'. As the French bangles at the foot of page 130 show, these were composed of twisted, three-dimensional forms, adorned with prominent bosses. The latter were probably intended as imitations of coral studs although, in some cases, they are reminiscent of bulging eyes. A number of impressive armlets have also been discovered in Scotland (page 130), indicating just how fecund the La Tène influence could be, even in its most outlying areas.

Perhaps the greatest glories of Celtic jewellery, though, were its brooches. Many of these evolved from the fibula, an ancient style of brooch resembling a safety pin. The basic function of the fibula was to fasten clothes together and, during the Celtic period, its bow became more pronounced, to enable it to hold a greater bulk of material. Sometimes a small triangular plate was used to strengthen the bow (page 140) and an increasing amount of ornamental detail was added to this arched section. The full range of La Tène motifs were employed, both abstract (page 138) and figurative. Many fibulae also featured a loop, as the Celts liked to wear them in pairs, attached with a chain.

Even though some fibulae were extremely ornate, their prestige has been eclipsed by the marvellous penannular brooches that were fashioned in Scotland and Ireland during the Christian era. Penannulars owed their name to the gap in their hoop and, initially, they too were designed as garment fasteners. Such practical considerations were soon overshadowed, however, giving way to a flaunting show of opulence. This reached a climax with the Tara brooch (page 135), where every square inch of space, both front and back, was covered with a virtuoso display of Celtic craftsmanship.

These pages include a number of brooches, buckles and belt-ornaments. The cross with the chain and inlaid enamel (facing page, centre, left) comes from La Gorge-Meillet in France.

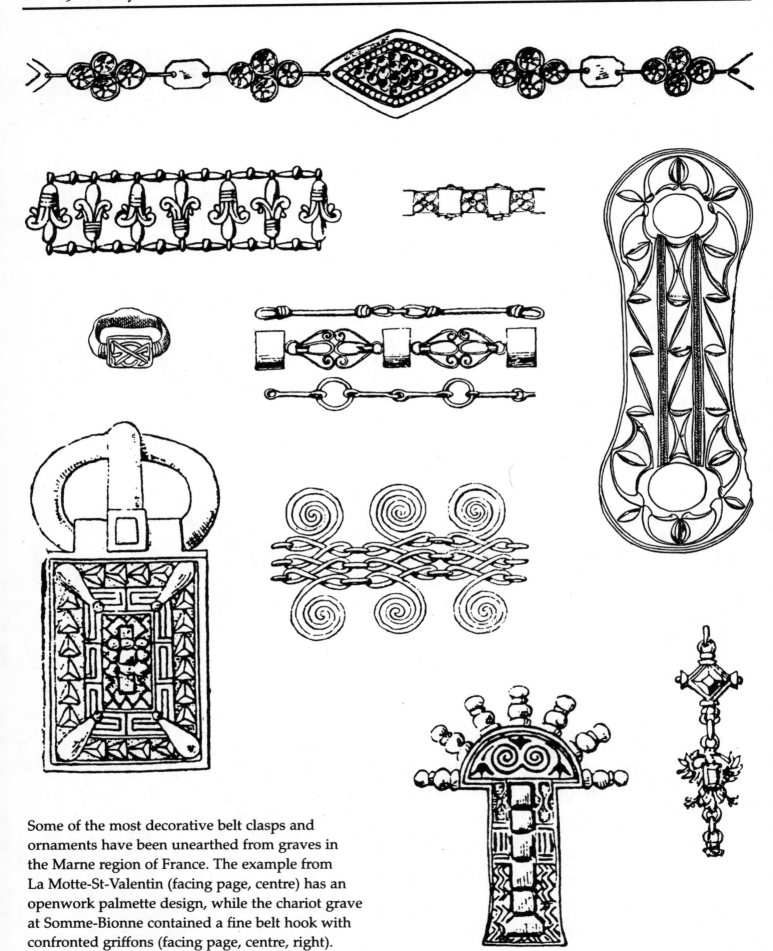

Some of the most decorative belt clasps and ornaments have been unearthed from graves in the Marne region of France. The example from La Motte-St-Valentin (facing page, centre) has an openwork palmette design, while the chariot grave at Somme-Bionne contained a fine belt hook with confronted griffons (facing page, centre, right).

The most lavish of these jewellery items are the gold lunula from Killarney, Co. Kerry (top, far right) and, below it, a golden diadem. The three necklets come from Elisried, and St. Germain and Delle in France, while the silver brooch (right) is from Goldsborough, N. Yorkshire.

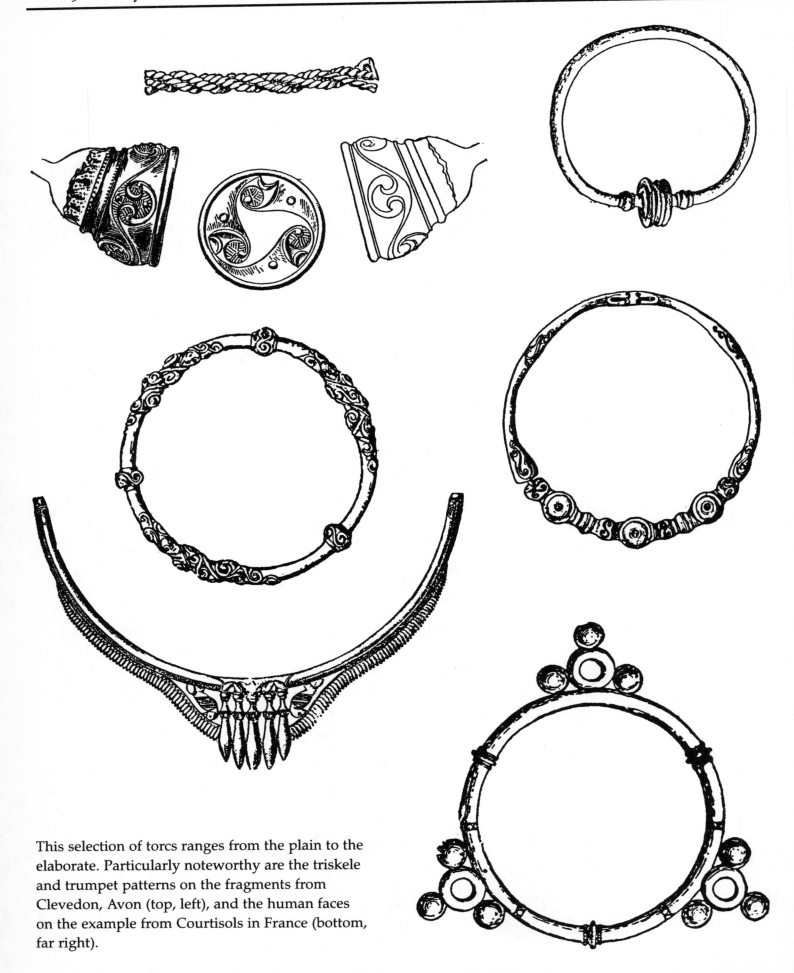

This selection of torcs ranges from the plain to the elaborate. Particularly noteworthy are the triskele and trumpet patterns on the fragments from Clevedon, Avon (top, left), and the human faces on the example from Courtisols in France (bottom, far right).

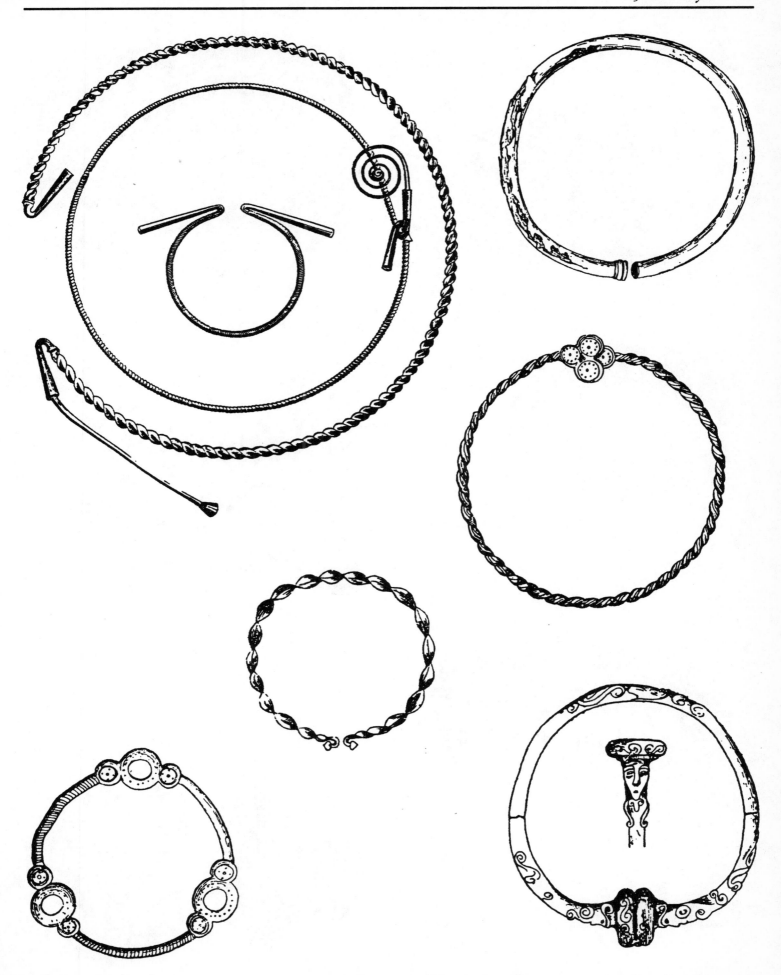

The most striking pieces from this group of armlets and bracelets come from Castle Newe, Grampian (above, right), and Plunton Castle, Dumfries & Galloway (top, right). The former features enamelled plaques with a red and yellow chequer pattern.

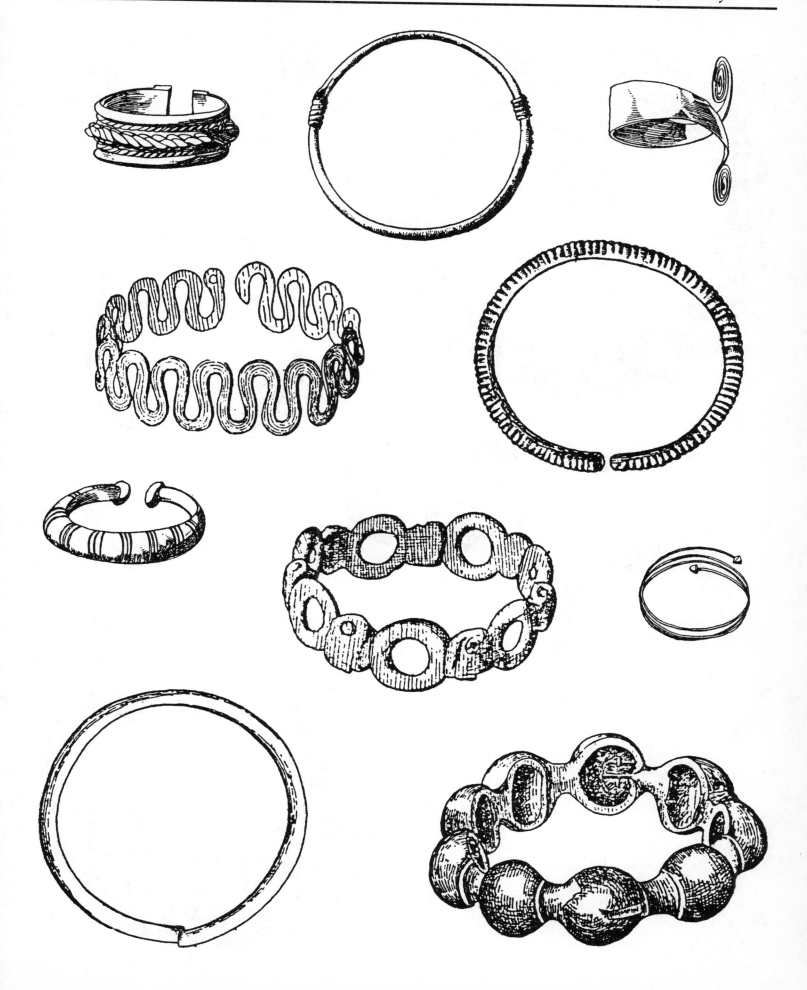

This is a rare example of a 'beaded' torc, from Lochar Moss, Dumfries & Galloway (top, far left). There is fine decoration, too, on the bracelets from Montsaugeon in France (facing page, centre, far right), Rodenbach in Germany (facing page, bottom, left), and Réallon, Hautes Alpes (right).

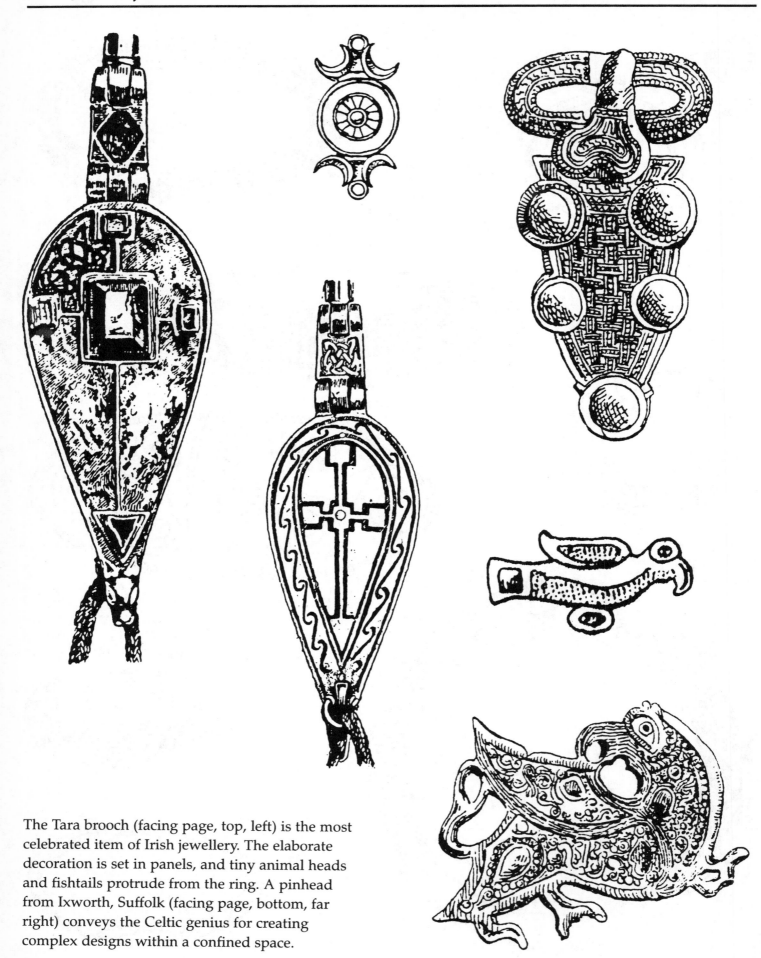

The Tara brooch (facing page, top, left) is the most celebrated item of Irish jewellery. The elaborate decoration is set in panels, and tiny animal heads and fishtails protrude from the ring. A pinhead from Ixworth, Suffolk (facing page, bottom, far right) conveys the Celtic genius for creating complex designs within a confined space.

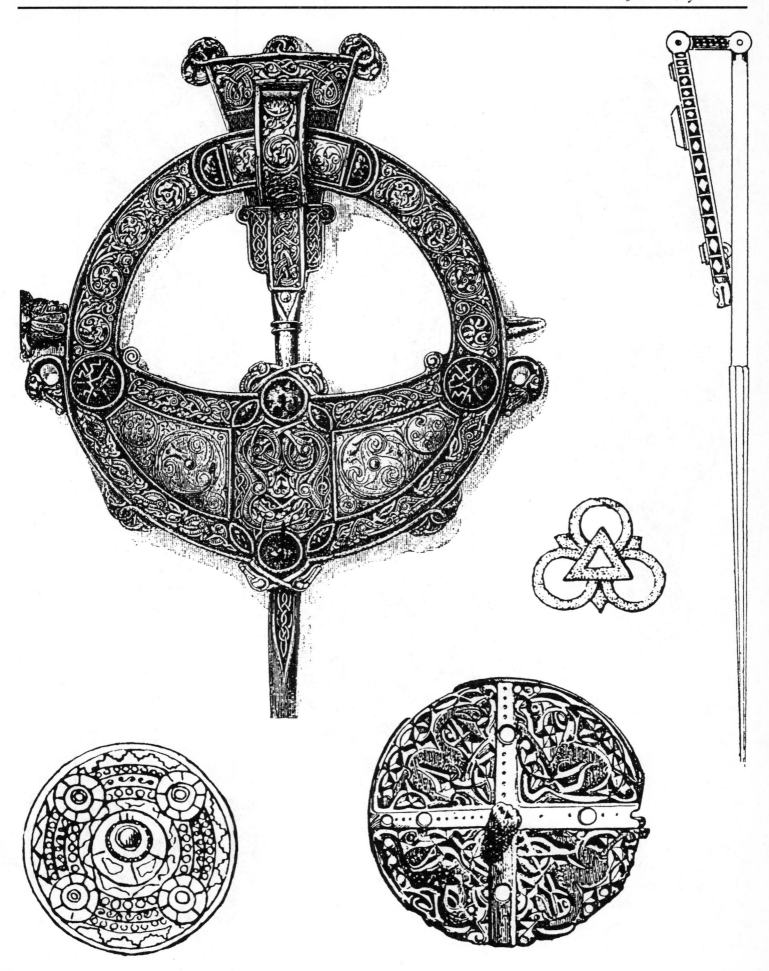

A selection of pins, pinheads and brooches. The large design on the facing page is an Irish penannular brooch with swivelling pin. The kite shaped brooch to the left of this is from Clonmacnois. In true Celtic fashion, the pendant terminates in a beast's head.

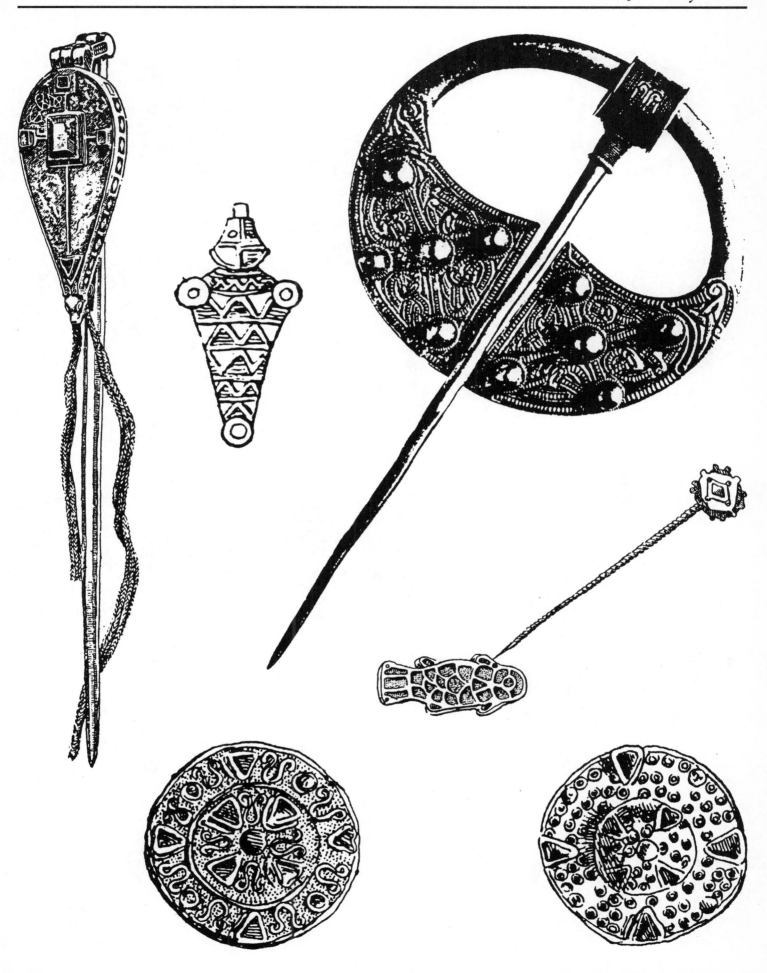

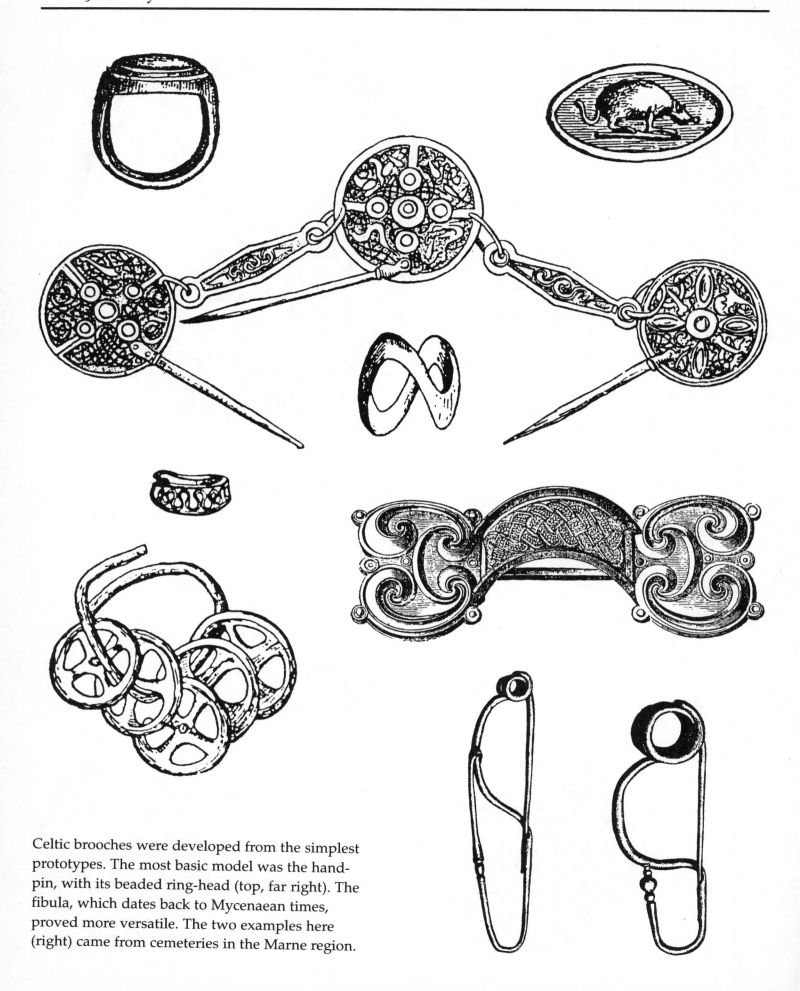

Celtic brooches were developed from the simplest prototypes. The most basic model was the hand-pin, with its beaded ring-head (top, far right). The fibula, which dates back to Mycenaean times, proved more versatile. The two examples here (right) came from cemeteries in the Marne region.

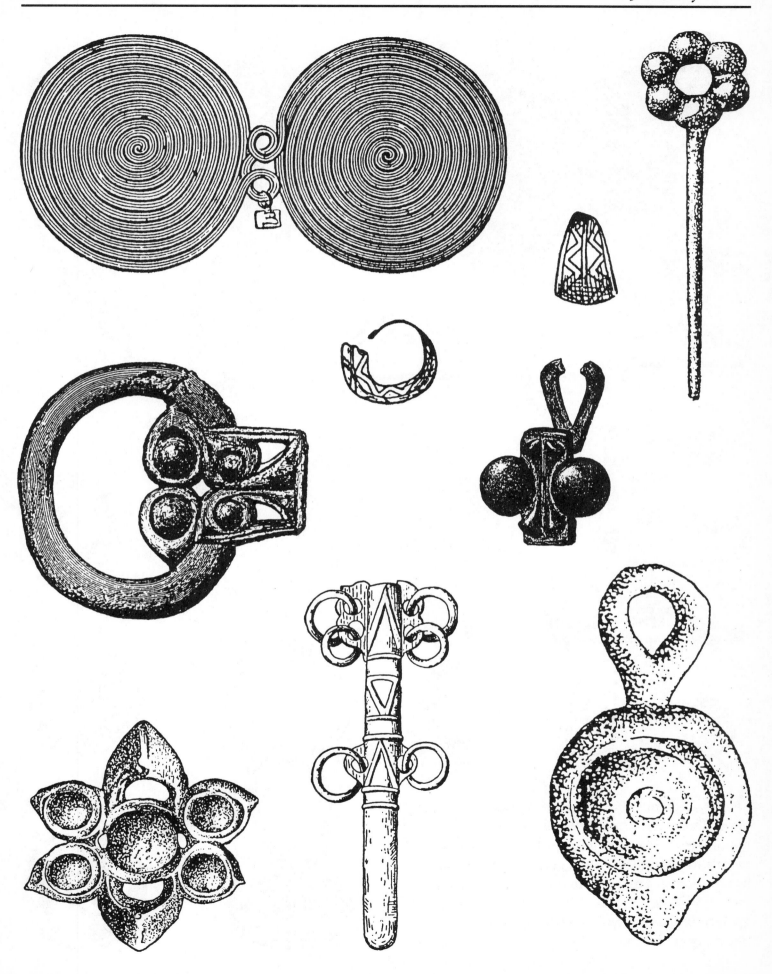

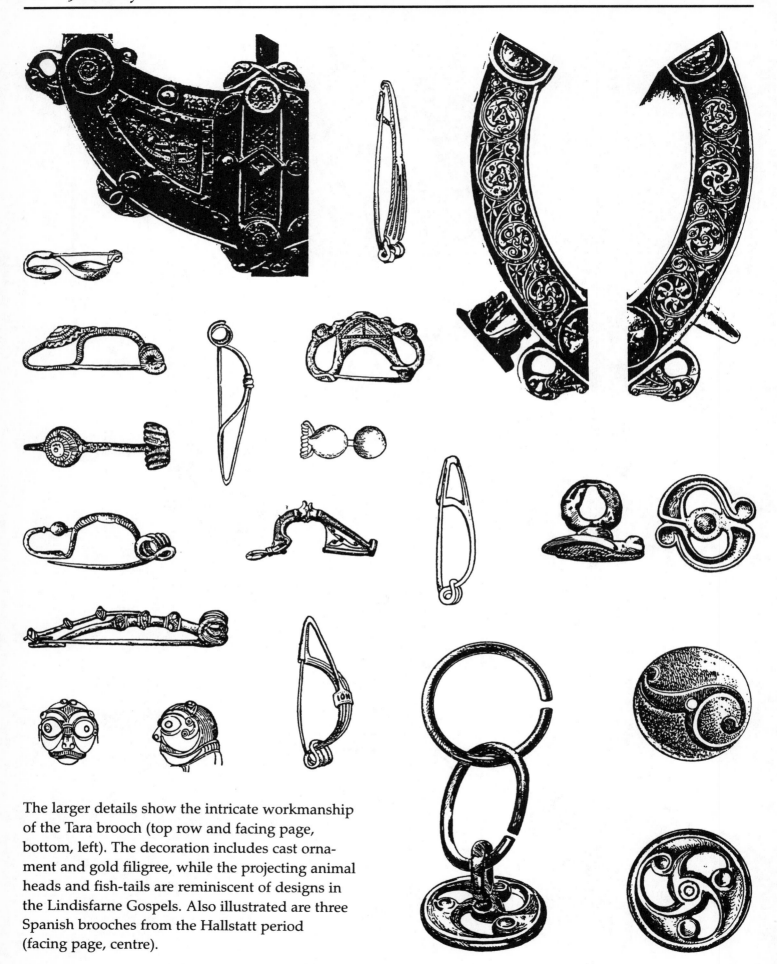

The larger details show the intricate workmanship of the Tara brooch (top row and facing page, bottom, left). The decoration includes cast ornament and gold filigree, while the projecting animal heads and fish-tails are reminiscent of designs in the Lindisfarne Gospels. Also illustrated are three Spanish brooches from the Hallstatt period (facing page, centre).

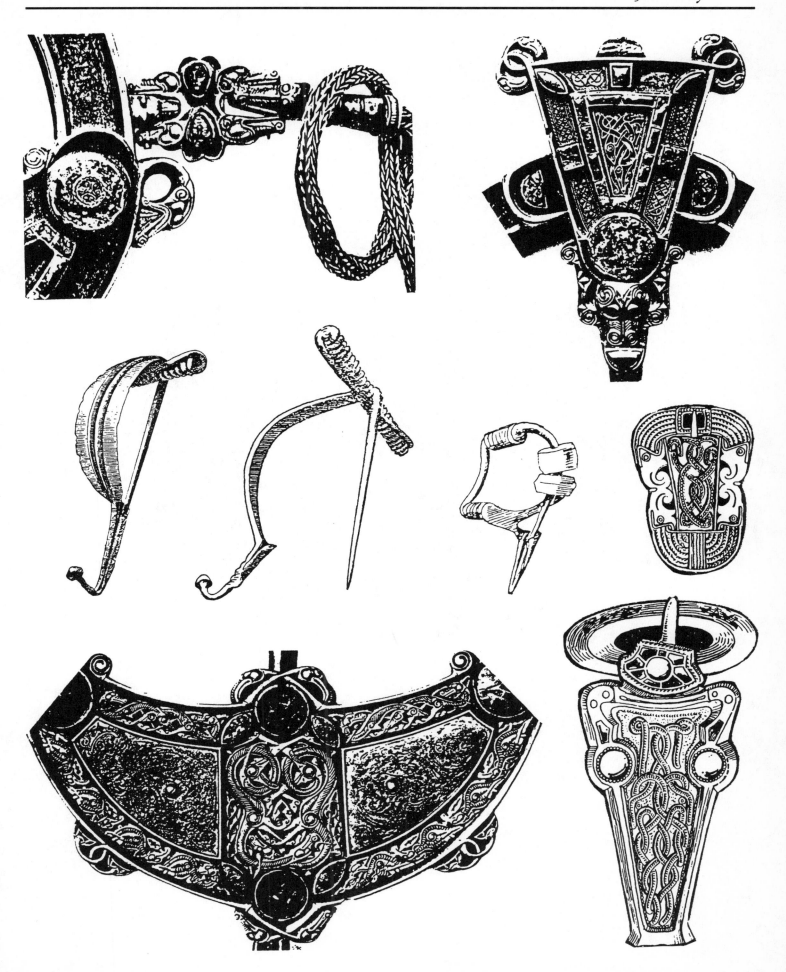

# Artefacts

The majority of artefacts from the La Tène period have survived in two distinct ways; either as grave goods, buried with their former owner, or as ritual offerings, thrown into rivers and lakes. In both cases, from the objects that have been discovered, it would seem that these were treasured possessions and the quality of the workmanship was correspondingly high.

This is particularly true of the fine, ceremonial armour and weaponry that has come to light. The Amfreville helmet (page 160), for example, was originally covered with a band of gold foil and enamel inlays, and would have been too precious to wear into battle. Other items, such as the Battersea shield and the Waterloo Bridge helmet (pages 160 and 161) are quite fragile and would not have withstood the rigours of armed combat.

Swords carried an even greater prestige and were often given a place of honour in the grave, close to the dead warrior's hand. As the Celts liked to fight with long, powerful swords, these needed to have sizeable hilts and so this area became the natural focus of decoration. Hence, the hat-shaped pommel of one early Hallstatt sword (page 156) was adorned with ivory and amber. On later swords and daggers, the hilts were often anthropomorphic (page 158). Warriors used the 'torsos' of these weapons as handgrips, while the head at the pommel may have had a talismanic significance.

A similar care was lavished on the ornamental fittings for chariots and harnesses. The most attractive of these were the enamelled bronze mounts, which were early versions of horse brasses. With their bright red inlays, the examples found at Polden Hill in Somerset (pages 148 and 149) are particularly colourful. The Torrs pony cap (page 149), discovered in a Scottish peat bog, is even more remarkable. The horns, however, have no historical connection with the piece and probably belonged to a set of drinking vessels.

In female graves, the emphasis was on jewellery and associated objects of beauty. Foremost among these were the fine bronze mirrors, which were particularly popular in Roman Britain. A rocked tracer (an engraving implement) created the flowing 'basketry' designs on mirror backs, that contrasted so effectively with the smooth areas of polished metal.

During the Christian era, a new range of artefacts was introduced by Irish craftsmen. Items such as chalices, croziers and patens were produced for normal liturgical use and are comparable with their Continental equivalents. Celtic shrines, however, were more distinctive. 'Cumdachs' were box-like receptacles, designed to house the great Gospel Books. The Soiscél Molaise (page 152), with its emblems of the four Evangelists, is one of the finest surviving examples. Others may have been even grander for, when the Book of Kells was stolen in 1007, thieves discarded the manuscript and made off with its golden covering.

A selection of vessels, including cinerary urns (above), beakers (right) and vases. Geometric designs were prevalent, but the vase and lid from St Pol-de-Léon in Brittany (facing page, centre, right) give a foretaste of the curvilinear La Tène style.

This page shows a variety of La Tène pottery. The facing page includes geometric Hallstatt vases (top, left), a 'pilgrim flask' (bottom, right), and the remains of a bronze hanging-bowl (top, right) from Cerrig-y-Drudion in Wales.

A variety of enamelware found in Britain.
Immediately above is a horse mount, found at
Polden Hill, Somerset. The two mounts at the foot
of the facing page come from the same hoard.

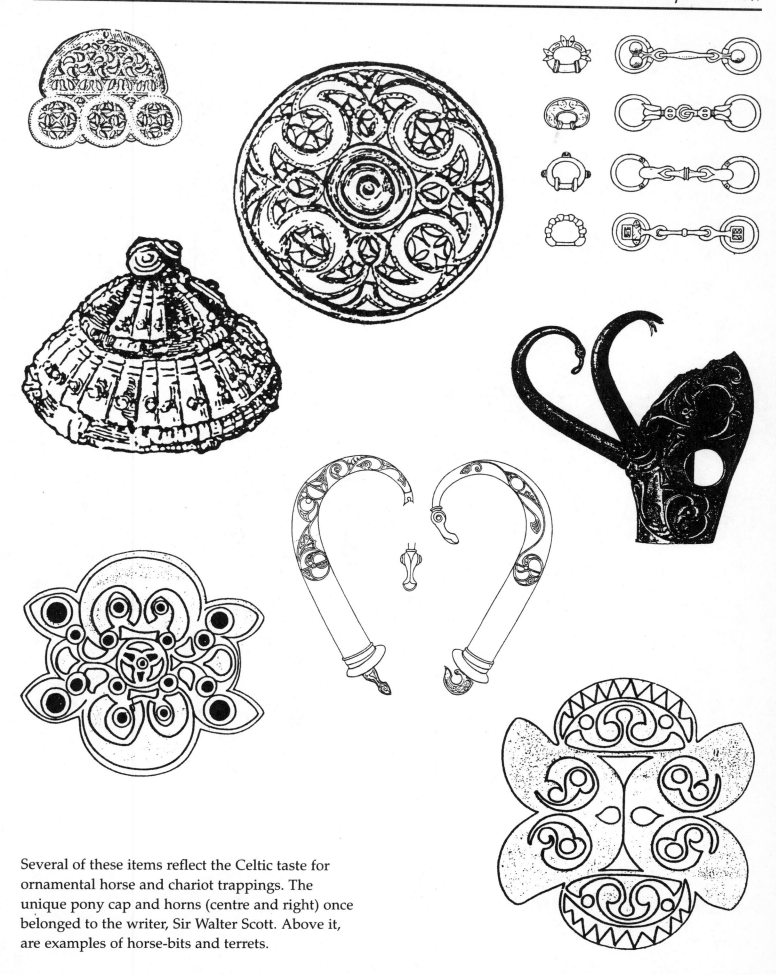

Several of these items reflect the Celtic taste for ornamental horse and chariot trappings. The unique pony cap and horns (centre and right) once belonged to the writer, Sir Walter Scott. Above it, are examples of horse-bits and terrets.

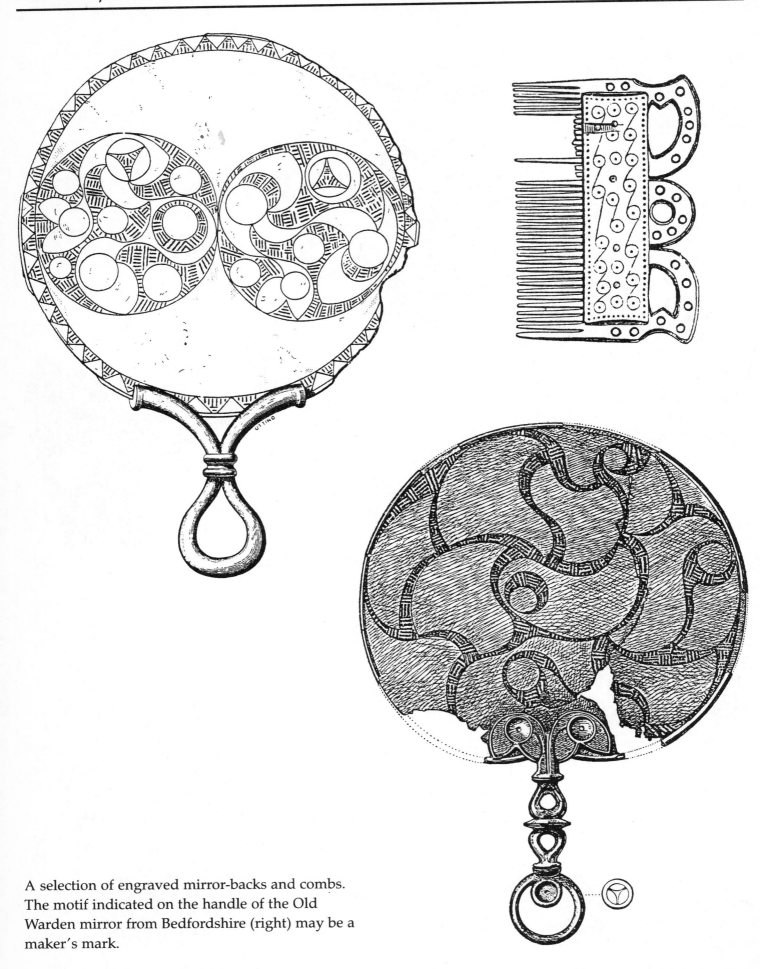

A selection of engraved mirror-backs and combs. The motif indicated on the handle of the Old Warden mirror from Bedfordshire (right) may be a maker's mark.

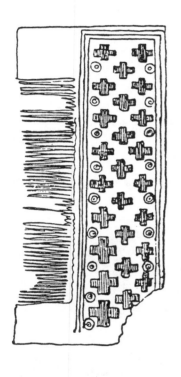

The mirror on the right comes from Nijmegen in Holland. Above it, an embossed plate from a mirror found at Balmaclellan in Scotland.

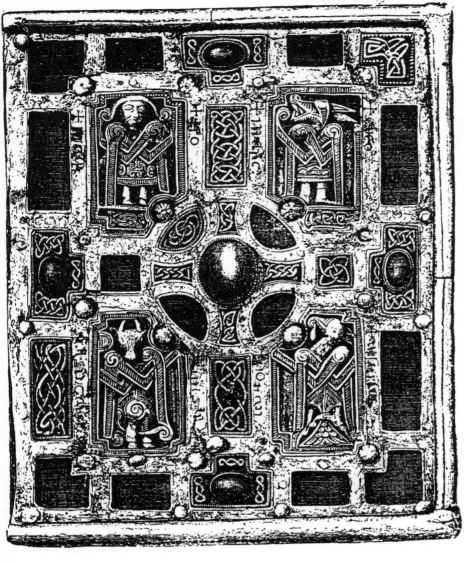

Some of the greatest glories of Celtic metalwork were produced for the Church. Pictured here are the shrine of St Patrick's Bell (facing page, centre, left), the Cross of Cong (right), the Clonmacnois Crozier (top, right), and the Soiscél Molaise (a book shrine, top left), all in the National Museum of Ireland, Dublin.

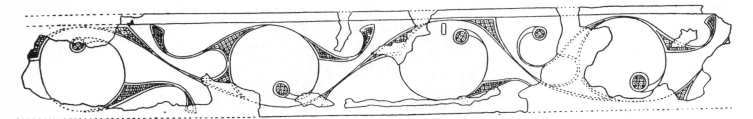

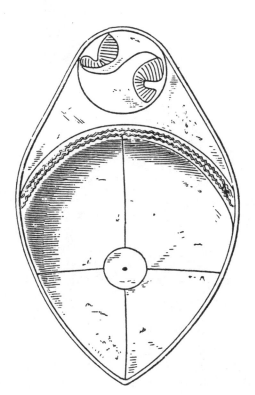

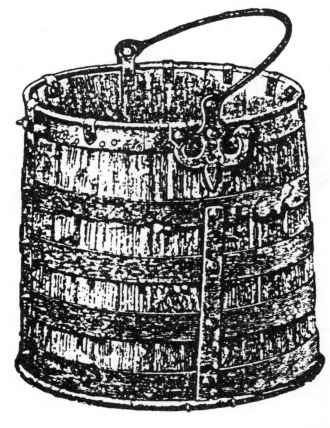

The two spoons are from Brickhill Lane, London (above) and from Crosby Ravensworth, Cumbria (above, right). The engraved decoration (top) is from a wooden tub found near Glastonbury, Somerset.

The Aylesford bucket from Kent (top, left) is notable for its stylized heads and the cavorting horses (centre), which feature on its ornamental repoussé band.

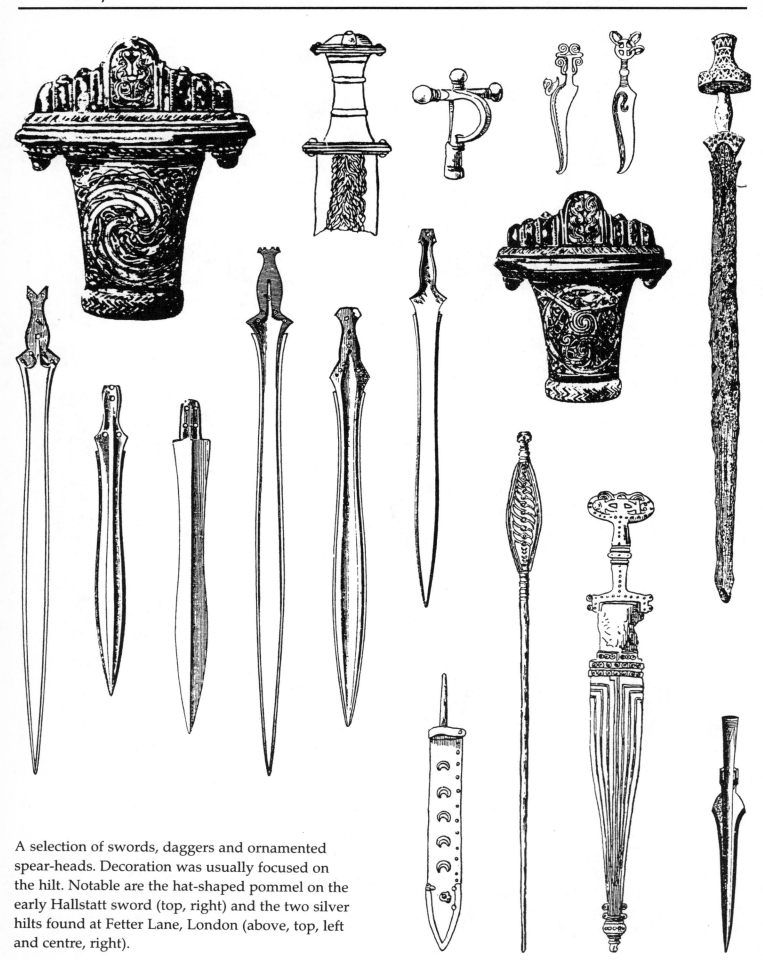

A selection of swords, daggers and ornamented spear-heads. Decoration was usually focused on the hilt. Notable are the hat-shaped pommel on the early Hallstatt sword (top, right) and the two silver hilts found at Fetter Lane, London (above, top, left and centre, right).

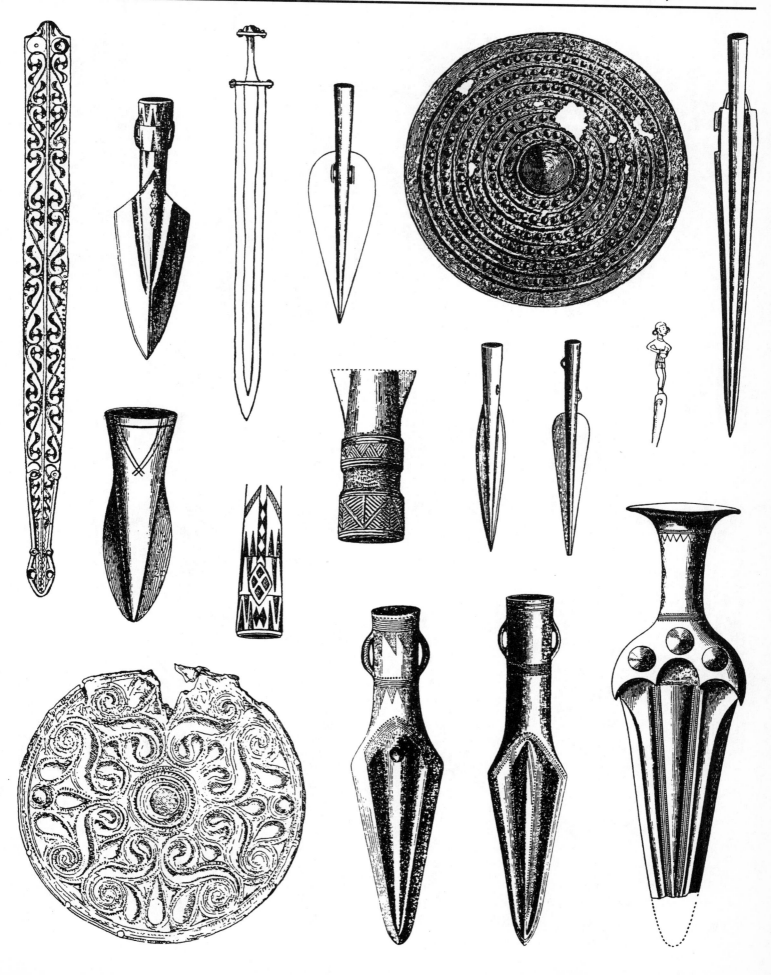

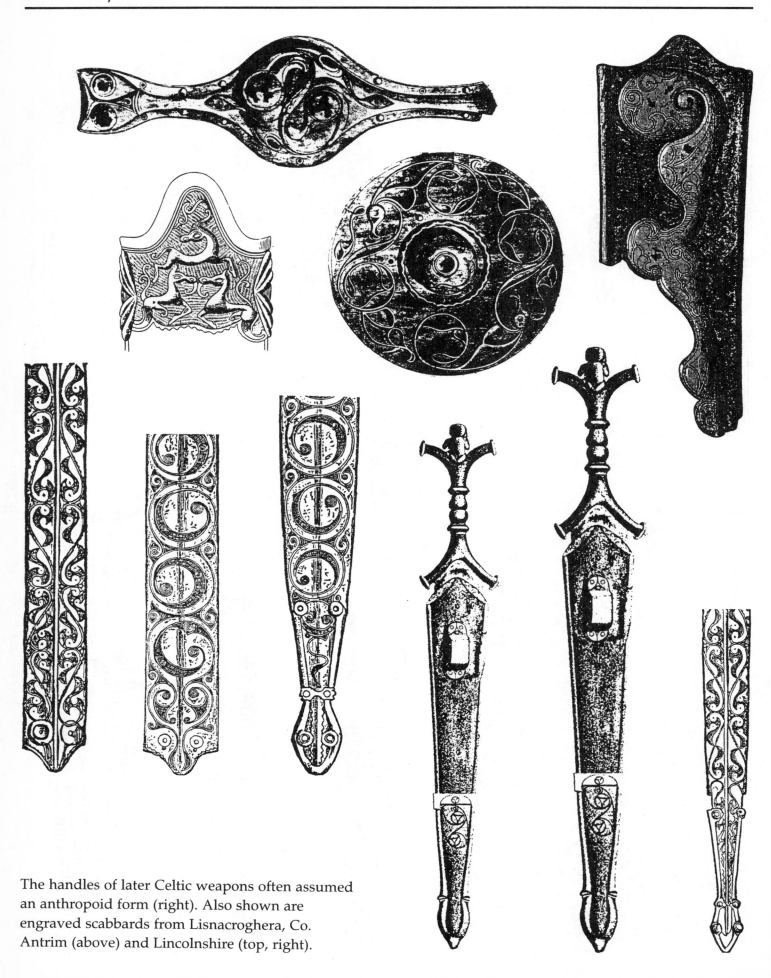

The handles of later Celtic weapons often assumed an anthropoid form (right). Also shown are engraved scabbards from Lisnacroghera, Co. Antrim (above) and Lincolnshire (top, right).

The decoration on most Celtic weaponry is abstract, but the bronze scabbard found in a Hallstatt grave (top, right) provides an obvious exception. Here, the most Celtic elements are the spiral haunches of the horses and the two-headed beast at the tip.

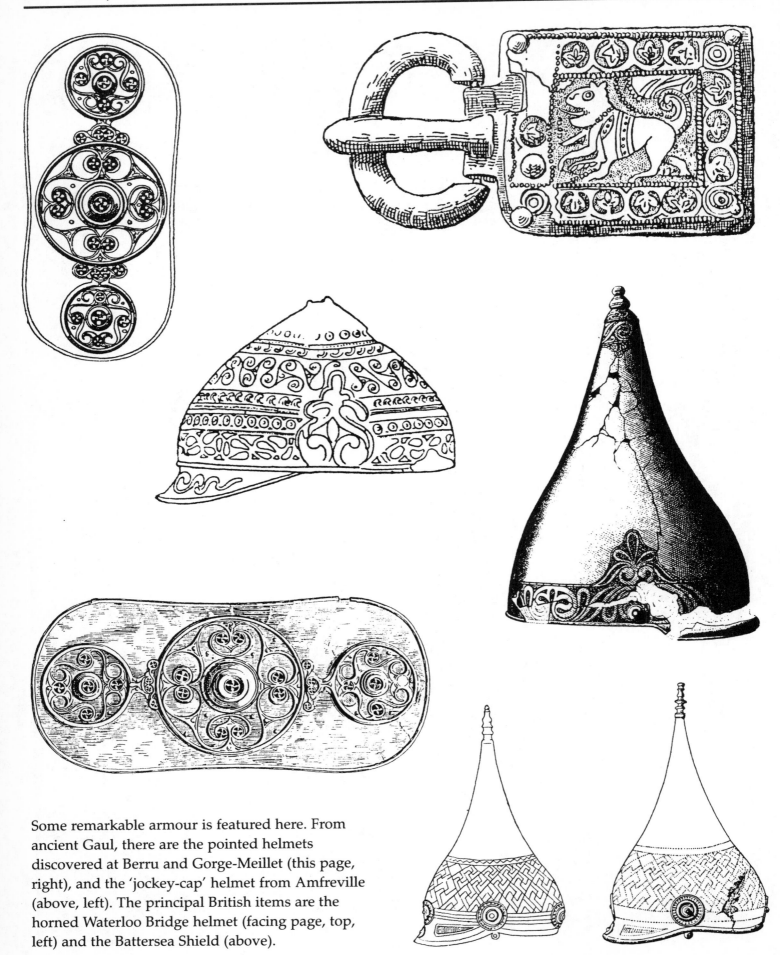

Some remarkable armour is featured here. From ancient Gaul, there are the pointed helmets discovered at Berru and Gorge-Meillet (this page, right), and the 'jockey-cap' helmet from Amfreville (above, left). The principal British items are the horned Waterloo Bridge helmet (facing page, top, left) and the Battersea Shield (above).

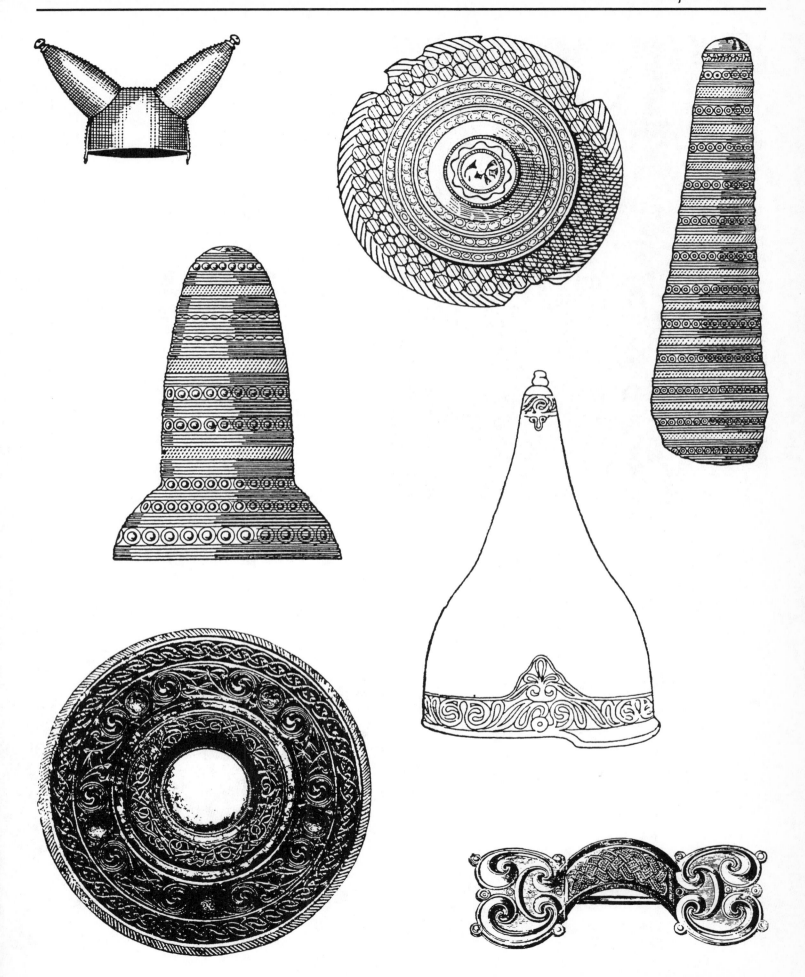

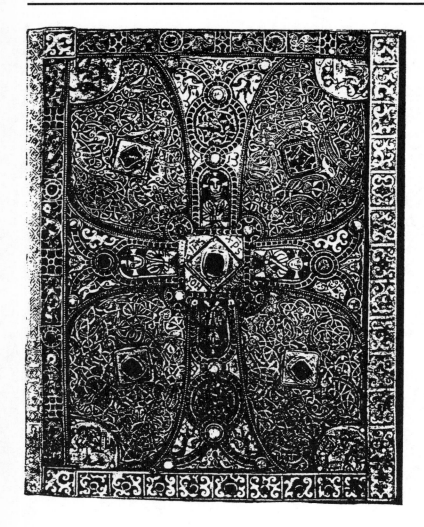

The Ardagh Chalice (right) is the finest example of
church plate to have survived the Viking raids in
Ireland. Above: a book cover from Lindau in
Germany and a Celtic harp.

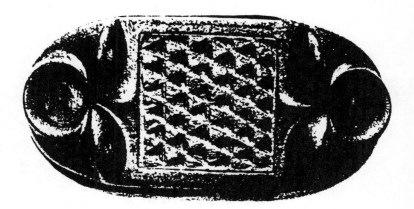

To the right: the remarkable, box-like shrine for
the Stowe Missal. Above: a silver pommel from
Windsor, Berks.

# Stonework

The marvellous High Crosses of Britain and Ireland provide one of the culminating triumphs of Celtic art and stem from a long tradition. Standing stones were commonplace in prehistoric Western Europe and the pagan Celts themselves erected their own monoliths. Remains of pillar statues, often surmounted with fearsome Janus heads, have been found near their shrines and burial places.

Despite the heathen associations of these monuments, the Christian missionaries sought to adapt rather than destroy them. This was done by carving simple crosses on the stones, a practice sanctioned by St Patrick. In time, converts began to create their own monuments and they naturally based these on the ancient models they saw around them. Hence, the earliest examples, like that at Reisk (page 174), consisted of rough slabs incised with Christian symbols. These were followed by carvings in low relief before eventually, the slabs themselves were sculpted into the shape of a cross. The monumental stone at Carndonagh (page 47) was one of the first of these.

Outdoor crosses served as meeting points for communal prayers and this accounts for the growing tendency to decorate them with scenes from the Scriptures. They effectively became visual aids for sermons, fulfilling the same function as stained glass in the Middle Ages. The most famous examples, at Monasterboice (pages 166 and 170) and Clonmacnois (page 177), were extremely ornate, but this narrative trend gradually led to a decline in the more abstract and stylized designs which had typified the La Tène style.

The erosion of the La Tène tradition can be seen even more clearly elsewhere. In Scotland, Celtic influences had increased after the early eighth century, when King Nechton imported artists from Northumbria. Pictish stonework, however, remained quite distinct. Symbols from the pagan era were retained (page 169) and the treatment of animals was more naturalistic (page 187). Pictish masons also preferred the slab format, placing most of their decoration around rather than on the cross.

In Ireland and northern England, Celtic designs were infiltrated by stylistic elements brought across by the Viking invaders. This is most apparent on artefacts such as the Clonmacnois Crozier (page 153), which displays the long curling tendrils that are characteristic of Ringerike, and also on English stonework. The images on pages 180 and 181 contain a number of Jellinge and Mammen motifs. Ribbon shaped animals encircled by strands of interlacing are common to both these styles, but the Mammen beast appears weightier and more powerful.

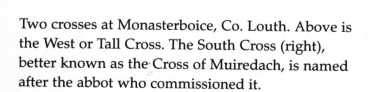

Two crosses at Monasterboice, Co. Louth. Above is
the West or Tall Cross. The South Cross (right),
better known as the Cross of Muiredach, is named
after the abbot who commissioned it.

The interlacing on these capitals at Killeshin
church, Co. Carlow, betrays a strong Celtic
influence, but no complete buildings in the
style have survived.

The spiral decoration at the passage-grave of
Newgrange, Co. Meath, pre dates the Celtic
era, but must have inspired its artists. Sunlight
penetrates the tomb at the winter solstice,
strengthening speculation that the spirals
have a cosmic significance.

Above: a Celtic cross at Irton, Cumbria. Right: an erect slab with Pictish symbols. The V and Z-shaped rods were common motifs, but their meaning remains obscure.

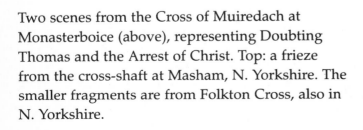

Two scenes from the Cross of Muiredach at Monasterboice (above), representing Doubting Thomas and the Arrest of Christ. Top: a frieze from the cross-shaft at Masham, N. Yorkshire. The smaller fragments are from Folkton Cross, also in N. Yorkshire.

The remains of the cross-shaft at Collingham, W. Yorkshire, are pictured above. Details of the sides are shown on the facing page (bottom, right) and here (centre). There are runic inscriptions on two of them (left and above).

There is a fine line between ornament and meaning in some Celtic stonework. Thus, in the Temptation of Adam and Eve (facing page, top, left), the Serpent and the Tree of Knowledge form part of the same knotwork design. Other figurative elements have no Biblical connection at all, such as the hunting scene from the cross at Ahenny, Co. Tipperary (facing page, bottom, left).

The incised design on a cross-slab at Reisk, Co. Kerry (above), shows an early form of the traditional Celtic cross. The North Cross at Ahenny, Co. Tipperary bears high relief carving (right).

Erect cross-slabs in Co. Donegal at Fahan Mura (above), and Carndonagh (right). Crosses were often formed out of knotwork, as the unbroken thread was thought to be a fitting symbol for the eternal journey of the spirit.

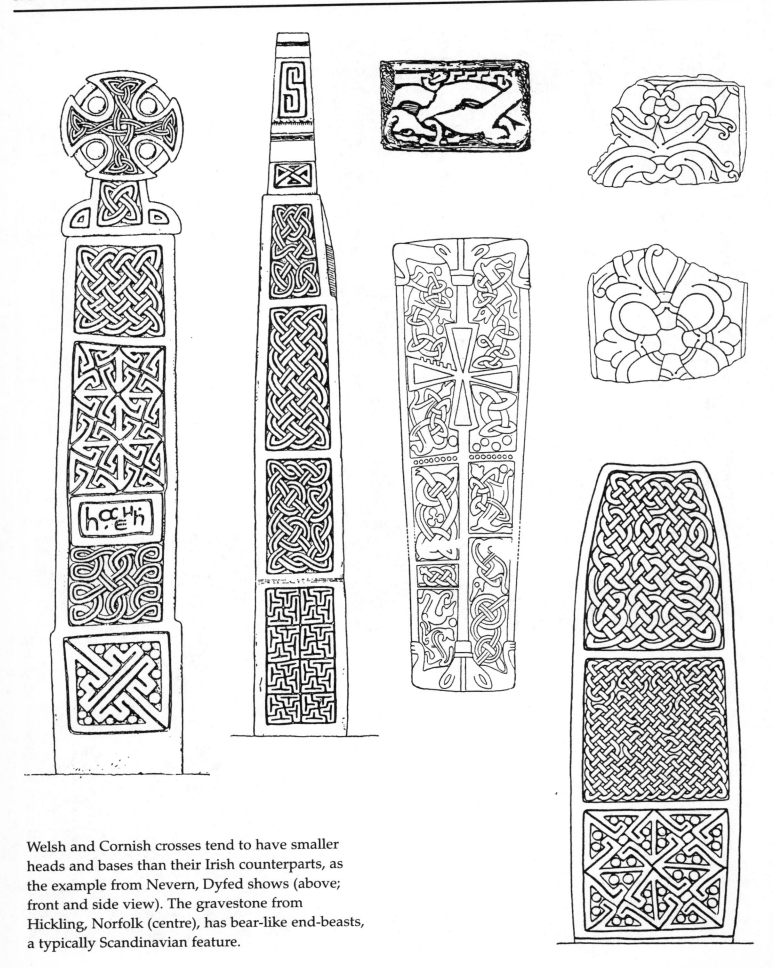

Welsh and Cornish crosses tend to have smaller
heads and bases than their Irish counterparts, as
the example from Nevern, Dyfed shows (above;
front and side view). The gravestone from
Hickling, Norfolk (centre), has bear-like end-beasts,
a typically Scandinavian feature.

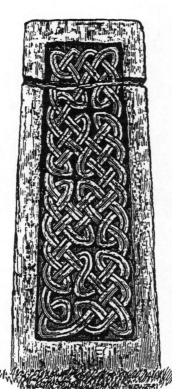

On the Cross of the Scriptures at Clonmacnois (centre), the subjects include the Last Judgement (within the circle) and depictions of Ciaran and Diarmuid, the founders of Clonmacnois (bottom panel). Directly above: Carew Cross, Dyfed. Right: a cross-shaft at Llantwit Major, S. Glamorgan.

Fragments from a selection of Anglian crosses and cross-shafts include a Scandinavian-style beast from Gainford, Durham (above). Next to it is a cross-head from Ellerburn. The carving at Sinnington (top, right) has been re-used in the nave of the church. Centre: details from the cross-shaft at Gilling. All three are from N. Yorkshire.

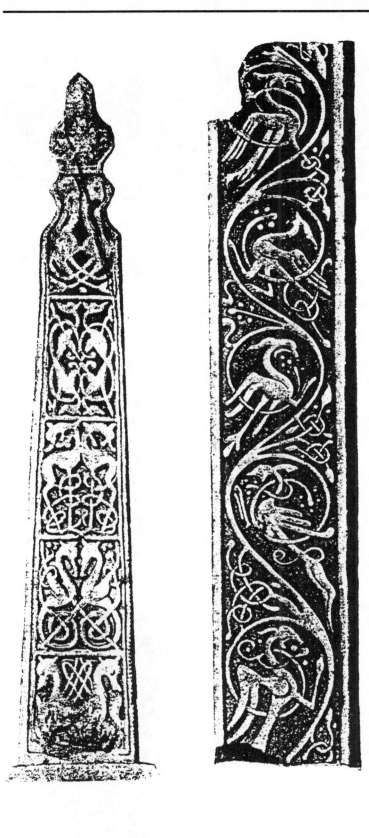

Right: two sides of the pedestal of Walton Cross in northern England. Centre: a border detail from the Pictish stone at Hilton of Cadboll, Highland. Confronted, ribbon-shaped beasts form the main decoration on Thornhill Cross in the north of Britain (left).

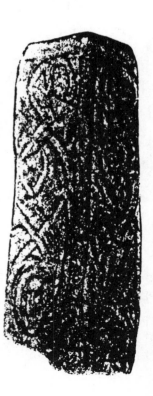

A limestone grave-cover from Levisham, N. Yorkshire (top), shows two sections of a ribbon-shaped beast, encircled by thick tendrils. The carving is heavily influenced by the Scandinavian Mammen style. The other details are from cross-shafts at Ilkley.

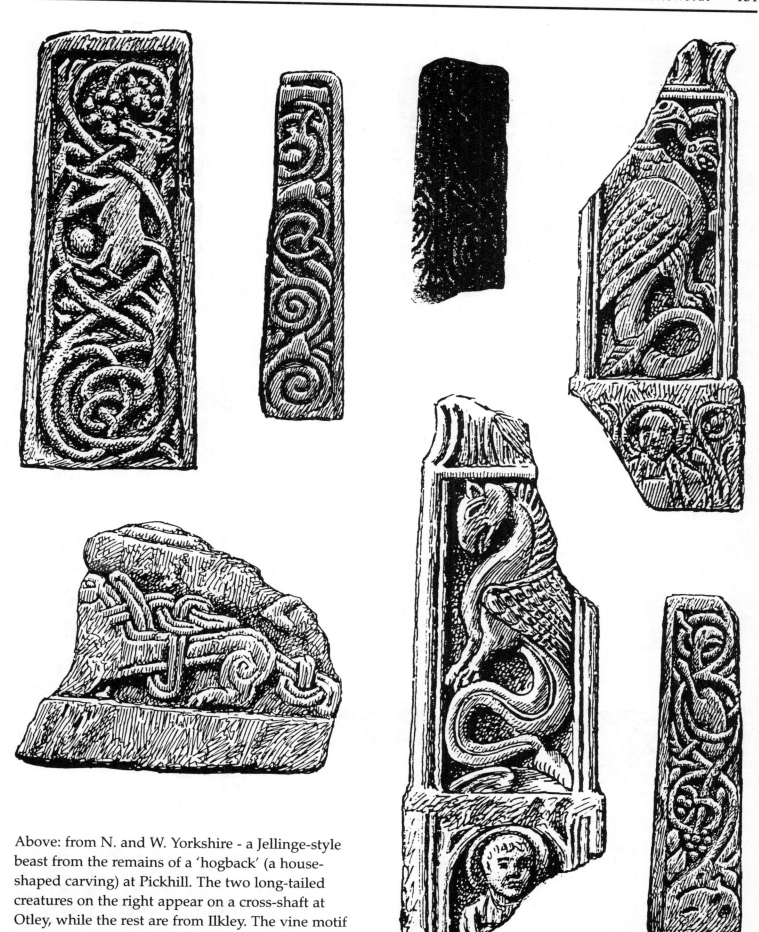

Above: from N. and W. Yorkshire - a Jellinge-style beast from the remains of a 'hogback' (a house-shaped carving) at Pickhill. The two long-tailed creatures on the right appear on a cross-shaft at Otley, while the rest are from Ilkley. The vine motif has Christian overtones.

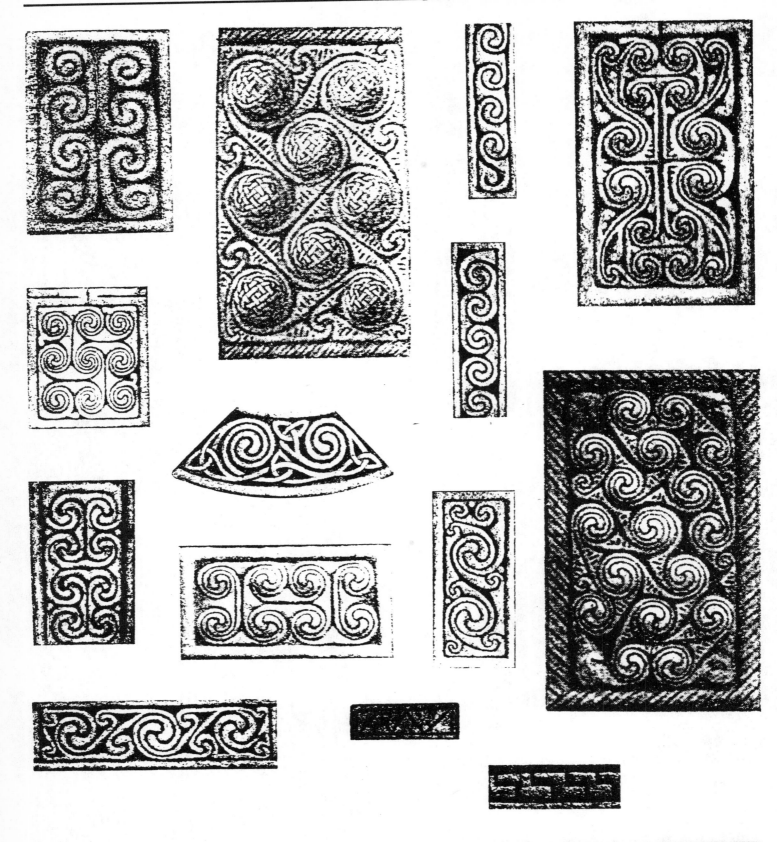

A selection of spirals and key patterns from Irish
and Pictish stonework. Crosses are often formed in
the breaks between these motifs (this page, top, right).

The centre of a wheel-cross usually featured a Last Judgement (facing page, bottom, left) on one side and a Crucifixion (top, left) on the other. Figurative details might convey other Biblical themes (e.g. the Twelve Apostles; facing page, left) or be purely ornamental (facing page, top row).

The broken grave slab (top, right) comes from Clonmacnois. The other monuments are from Wales. From the left, they are Penmon Cross, Eiudon's cross-shaft at Golden Grove, and the Wheel-cross of Conbelin at Margam Abbey. The latter's shaft has been shortened through damage.

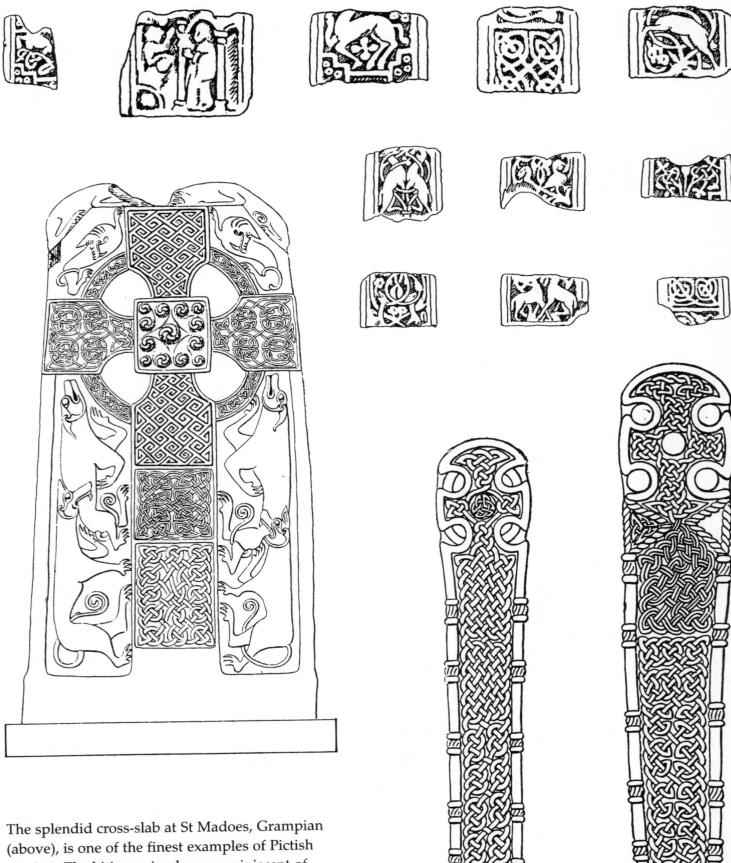

The splendid cross-slab at St Madoes, Grampian (above), is one of the finest examples of Pictish carving. The biting animals are reminiscent of manuscript illuminations. Right: the cross at Neuadd Siarman in Wales. Top: fragments of a cross-shaft at Aldborough, N. Yorkshire.

Two notable cross-slab designs are pictured here. These come from Clonmacnois (top, left) and Iniscaltra, Co. Clare (centre). Symbolic footprints are carved on the latter, indicating that this is the grave of someone who died while on a pilgrimage.

Recumbent cross-slabs were the forerunners of headstones. They were much more common in Ireland than elsewhere in Britain, and the largest collection of Celtic examples is at Clonmacnois. Above: a restored slab at Fuerty, Co. Roscommon.

A collection of erect and recumbent cross-slabs. One of the finest is that marking the tomb of St Berechtir at Tullylease, Co. Cork (top, far right). Many graves had inscriptions calling for prayers for the deceased ('Oroit...' often shortened to O̅R̅).

# Bibliography

ARNOLD, Bruce, *Irish Art*, Thames & Hudson, 1977

BACKHOUSE, Janet, *The Lindisfarne Gospels*, Phaidon, 1981

BAILEY, Richard N., *Viking Age of Sculpture in Northern England*, Collins, 1980

BAIN, George, *Celtic Art; the Methods of Construction*, Constable, 1994

BRYCE, Derek, *Symbolism of the Celtic Cross*, Llanerch Press, 1994

ELUERE, Christiane, *The Celts, First Masters of Europe*, Thames & Hudson, 1993

FINLAY, Ian, *Celtic Art*, Faber & Faber Ltd, 1973

GREEN, Miranda J., *Dictionary of Celtic Myth and Legend*, Thames & Hudson, 1992

HENDERSON, George, *From Durrow to Kells: The Insular Gospel Books 650-800*, Thames & Hudson, 1987

HENRY, Francoise, *Irish Art during the Viking Invasions (800-1020 AD)*, Methuen, 1967

LAING, Lloyd & Jennifer, *Art of the Celts*, Thames & Hudson, 1992

LAING, Lloyd, *Celtic Britain*, Granada, 1979

MACGOWAN, Kenneth, *Clonmacnois*, Kamad Publications, 1985

MEEHAN, Aidan, *Knotwork, the Secret Method of Scribes*, Thames & Hudson, 1991

MEEHAN, Aidan, *Animal Patterns*, Thames & Hudson, 1992

MEGAW, Ruth & Vincent, *Celtic Art*, Thames & Hudson, 1989

PIGGOTT, Stuart, *The Druids*, Thames & Hudson, 1975

RITCHIE, Anna, *Picts*, H.M.S.O., Edinburgh, 1989

ROMILLY Allen J., *Celtic Art*, Bracken Books, 1993

ROSS, Anne, *Pagan Celtic Britain*, Constable, 1967

RYAN, Dr Michael, *Metal Craftsmanship in Early Ireland*, Country House, 1993

SANDARS, N. K., *Prehistoric Art in Europe*, Pelican History of Art, 1968

SULLIVAN, Sir Edward, *The Book of Kells*, Studio Editions, 1986